E. L. PARKER & CO.

Importers and Dealers in

Tin Plate, Block Tin,

Hoop and Sheet Iron,

Zinc, Wire, Spelter,

Solder, Rivets, &c.

Tinners' Tools and Supplies.

Stamped, French and Japanned Ware,
And House Furnishing Goods of this Class Generally,
&c.

No. 83 South Charles Street,
Baltimore.
1868

The Toolemera Press
History Preserved
www.toolemerapress.com

E. 3L. Parker & Co.
Importers And Dealers In Tin Plate, Block Tin, Hoop And Sheet Iron, Zinc, Wire, Spelter, Solder, Rivets, &c. Tinners' Tools And Supplies. Stamped, French And Japanned Ware, And House Furnishing Goods Of This Class Generally, &c.
No. 83 South Charles Street
Baltimore (Maryland)
1868

No part of this book may be reproduced, stored in an electronic retrieval system, or transmitted in any form or by an means, electronic, mechanical, photocopy, photographic or otherwise without the written permission of the publisher.

Excerpts of one page or less for the purposes of review and comment are permissible.

Copyright © 2019 The Toolemera Press
All rights reserved.

International Standard Book Number
ISBN : 978-1-0878-1237-3
(Trade Paperback)

Published by
Gary Roberts DBA The Toolemera Press
Wilmington, North Carolina
U.S.A. 28412

https://toolemerapress.com

Manufactured in the United States of America

Toolemera Press Reprints

Founded in 1849 and in business through the turn of the century, E. L. Parker & Co. of Baltimore, Maryland was a major importer and wholesaler of tin plate, sheet iron and related metals, General Store hard goods and Tinners (Tinsmith) tools and machinery.

"It's reputation and sales are widespread and it has important connections in England, as well as with the best firms of Maryland, Virginia, West Virginia, Pennsylvania, North and South Carolina, Georgia, Alabama and Tennessee." Baltimore: It's History And It's People. Vol. II Biography, page 335.

The E. L. Parker & Co. 1868 trade catalog is reproduced in facsimile from the original held in the collection of Gary Roberts, Publisher, The Toolemera Press.

The Toolemera Press imprint, re-publishes classic books on early crafts, trades and industries, from his personal library.

www.toolemerapress.com
History Preserved

E. L. PARKER & CO.

Importers and Dealers in

Tin Plate, Block Tin,

Hoop and Sheet Iron,

ZINC, WIRE, SPELTER,

SOLDER, RIVETS, &c.

Tinners' Tools and Supplies.

—— ALSO ——

Stamped, French and Japanned Ware,

And House Furnishing Goods of this Class Generally, &c.

No. 83 South Charles Street,

BALTIMORE.

1868.

MURPHY & CO., Printers, Baltimore.

TIN PLATE, SHEET IRON, WIRE, METALS,

&c., &c.

TRUNK HOOPS.

7/8 inch wide. . . .	Thickness No. 22.	Wire Guage.
1 "	" 22.	"
1 1/8 "	" 22.	"
1 1/4 "	" 22.	"

GALVANIZED HOOP IRON.

1/2 inch wide. . .	Thickness No. 22. . .	Wire Guage.	cts. per pound.
5/8 "	" 22. . .	"	" "
3/4 "	" 20. . .	"	" "
7/8 "	" 19. . .	"	" "
1 "	" 19. . .	"	" "
1 1/8 "	" 18. . .	"	" "
1 1/4 "	" 18. . .	"	" "
1 1/2 "	" 18. . .	"	" "
1 3/4 "	" 17. . .	"	" "
2 "	" 15. . .	"	" "

ROUND IRON.

IN 56 LB. BUNDLES.

3-16 in.	per ton.	per bdl.
1-4 in.	"	"
5-16 in.	"	"

SHEET ZINC.

24, 30, 32, 34, 36, 40 inches wide by 7 feet long.

No. 9, weighs 11 ounces per square foot.	No. 11, weighs 15 ounces per square foot.
10, " 13 " "	12, " 17 1/2 " "

COPPER.

Copper in bolts, . . .	1/4 to 2 in.	
" " sheets, . . .	30 by 60 inches. . . .	Any thickness.
" " " . . .	14 by 48 " . . .	12 to 20 oz.

TINNED COPPER.

14 x 48 in. .	14 and 16 oz. per sq. foot. .	Tinning per sheet. . .
30 x 60 in. .	9 and 10 lbs. per sheet. .	" " . .

BLOCK TIN IN PIGS.

English, ...
Straits, ...
Banca, ...

BLOCK TIN IN BARS.

CHARCOAL TIN PLATE.

IC	10 by 14 inches.	225 sheets in each box.	
IX	10 by 14 "	225 "	"
IXX	10 by 14 "	225 "	"
IXXX	10 by 14 "	225 "	"
ICW	10 by 14 "	225 "	"
IXW	10 by 14 "	225 "	"
IC	12 by 12 "	225 "	"
IX	12 by 12 "	225 "	"
IXX	12 by 12 "	225 "	"
IXXX	12 by 12 "	225 "	"
IX	14 by 14 "	225 "	"
DC	12½ by 17 "	100 "	"
DX	12½ by 17 "	100 "	"
DXX	12½ by 17 "	100 "	"
DXXX	12½ by 17 "	100 "	"
SDC	11 by 15 "	200 "	"
SDX	11 by 15 "	200 "	"
IC	14 by 20 "	112 "	"
IX	14 by 20 "	112 "	"
IXX	14 by 20 "	112 "	"
IXXX	14 by 20 "	112 "	"
IXXXX	14 by 20 "	112 "	"
IC	20 by 28 "	56 & 112 "	"
IX	20 by 28 "	56 & 112 "	"

COKE TIN PLATE.

ALL GRADES.

IC	10 by 14 inches.	225 sheets in each box.	
IC	12 by 12 "	225 "	"
IC	14 by 20 "	112 "	"

ROOFING PLATE.

IC	Terne or Leaded.	14 by 20 inches.	112 sheets in each box.	
IX	" "	14 by 20 "	112 "	"

NEW SIZE ROOFING PLATE.

IC	Terne or Leaded.	20 by 28 inches.	56 & 112 sheets in each box.	
IX	" "	20 by 28 "	56 & 112 "	"

TAGGER'S TIN.

10 by 14 inches. . . . TTT . . . 450 sheets in each box.

Tinned Iron for Cotton Cans.

AMERICAN SHEET IRON.

COMMON AND BEST.

Common.—Nos. 20, 21, 22, 23, 24, 25, 26, 27 and 28.—24 inches wide, by 7 to 9 feet long, ...

Annealed.—Nos. 12, 13, 14, 15, 16, 17, 18.—24 to 30 inches wide, by 7 to 9 feet long, ...

Best Refined "Octoraro" Patent Cleaned.—Nos. 14, 15, 16, 17, 18, 19, 20, 21, 22, 23, 24, 25, 26, 27 and 28.—24 to 30 inches wide, by 7 to 8 feet long, ...

Extra sizes made to order.   Over 30 inches wide, extra price.

RUSSIA SHEET IRON.

No.	Size	Weight
8,	28 by 56 inches,	weighs about 7 pounds per sheet.
9,	28 by 56 "	" " 8 " "
10,	28 by 56 "	" " 9 " "
11,	28 by 56 "	" " 10 " "
12,	28 by 56 "	" " 11 " "
13,	28 by 56 "	" " 12 " "
14,	28 by 56 "	" " 13 " "
15,	28 by 56 "	" " 14 " "
16,	28 by 56 "	" " 15 " "

IMITATION RUSSIA SHEET IRON.

No.	Size	Weight
27,	28 by 56 inches,	weighs about 8 pounds per sheet.
26,	28 by 56 "	" " 9 " "
25,	28 by 56 "	" " 10 " "
24,	28 by 56 "	" " 11 " "
23,	28 by 56 "	" " 12 " "
22,	28 by 56 "	" " 13 " "
21,	28 by 56 "	" " 14 " "
20,	28 by 56 "	" " 15 " "

AMERICAN GALVANIZED SHEET IRON.

From Nos. 14 to 28 inclusive.   Ordinary Sizes 24 to 30 inches wide, and 6 to 8 feet long.

Nos. 14 to 20, . . W. G. inclusive, . . cts. per pound.
     21 to 24, . . " . . " "
     25 & 26, . . " . . " "
     27, . . . " . . " "
     28, . . . " . . " "

Under 24 or over 30 inches wide, and pattern lengths, will be charged extra, according to the size required.

TABLE *showing the comparative Weight and Measurement of Galvanized Sheet Iron. Size of sheet, 2 feet wide by from 6 to 9 feet long.*

No. Wire Guage.	Weight per square foot.	Square feet per ton.
30	10 oz.	about 3,584.
29	11 "	" 3,280.
28	12 "	" 2,986.
27	14 "	" 2,685.
26	15 "	" 2,389.
25	16 "	" 2,248.
24	17 "	" 2,108.
23	19 "	" 1,907.
22	21 "	" 1,706.
21	24 "	" 1,493.
20	28 "	" 1,280.
19	33 "	" 1,124.
18	37 "	" 968.
17	43 "	" 857.
16	48 "	" 746.
15	54 "	" 661.
14	60 "	" 594.

HOOP IRON.

Width		Thickness	Wire Guage.
½ inch wide.		No. 22.	"
⅝ "		" 22.	"
¾ "		" 20.	"
⅞ "		" 19.	"
1 "		" 19.	"
1⅛ "		" 18.	"
1¼ "		" 18.	"
1½ "		" 16 to 18.	"
1¾ "		" 15 to 17.	"
2 "		" 14	"

TRUNK HOOPS.

7/8 inch wide.	Thickness No. 22.	Wire Guage.
1 "	" 22.	"
1 1/8 "	" 22.	"
1 1/4 "	" 22.	"

GALVANIZED HOOP IRON.

1/2 inch wide.	Thickness No. 22.	Wire Guage.	cts. per pound.
5/8 "	" 22.	"	" "
3/4 "	" 20.	"	" "
7/8 "	" 19.	"	" "
1 "	" 19.	"	" "
1 1/8 "	" 18.	"	" "
1 1/4 "	" 18.	"	" "
1 1/2 "	" 18.	"	" "
1 3/4 "	" 17.	"	" "
2 "	" 15.	"	" "

ROUND IRON.

IN 56 LB. BUNDLES.

3-16 in.	per ton.	per bdl.
1-4 in.	"	"
5-16 in.	"	"

SHEET ZINC.

24, 30, 32, 34, 36, 40 inches wide by 7 feet long.

No. 9, weighs 11 ounces per square foot.	No. 11, weighs 15 ounces per square foot.
10, " 13 " "	12, " 17 1/2 " "

COPPER.

Copper in bolts,	1/4 to 2 in.	
" " sheets,	30 by 60 inches.	Any thickness.
" " "	14 by 48 "	12 to 20 oz.

TINNED COPPER.

14 x 48 in.	14 and 16 oz. per sq. foot.	Tinning per sheet.
30 x 60 in.	9 and 10 lbs. per sheet.	" "

BLOCK TIN IN PIGS.

English,
Straits,
Banca,

BLOCK TIN IN BARS.

Iron Wire.

Bright, Annealed and Copper Coated.

In Bundles of 63 lbs. each.

	Cents.		Feet.
No. 00, List per lb.	9	Length of 1 bdl.	171
0, " "	9	" 1 "	213
1, " "	9	" 1 "	273
2, " "	9	" 1 "	315
3, " "	9	" 1 "	363
4, " "	9	" 1 "	429
5, " "	9	" 1 "	510
6, " "	9	" 1 "	609
7, " "	10	" 1 "	717
8, " "	10	" 1 "	858
9, " "	10	" 1 "	1026
10, " "	11	" 1 "	1260
11, " "	11	" 1 "	1587
12, " "	$11\frac{1}{2}$	" 1 "	2100
13, " "	$12\frac{1}{2}$	" 1 "	2679
14, " "	$12\frac{1}{2}$	" 1 "	3426
15, " "	14	" 1 "	4404
16, " "	14	" 1 "	5862
17, " "	15	" 1 "	7620
18, " "	16	" 1 "	9450
19, " "	19	" 1 "	12,255

WIRE IN STONES.

Of 12 Pounds each.

BRIGHT AND ANNEALED.

No. 20, List per lb.	20 cents.	No. 29, List per lb.	30 cents.
21, " "	21 "	30, " "	32 "
22, " "	22 "	31, " "	33 "
23, " "	23 "	32, " "	35 "
24, " "	24 "	33, " "	37 "
25, " "	25 "	34, " "	40 "
26, " "	26 "	35, " "	45 "
27, " "	28 "	36, " "	55 "
28, " "	29 "		

GALVANIZED WIRE.

WITH ZINC.

Nos. 0, 1, 2, 3, 4, 5, 6, 7, 8, 9, 10, 11, 12, 13, 14, 15, 16, 17, 18.

RYLAND'S
English Tinned Iron Wire,

IN BUNDLES OF 63 POUNDS EACH.

From Nos. 3 up to 19, inclusive.

TINNED BROOM WIRE.

Nos. 20, 21 and 22, ... per lb.

PIG LEAD.   *BAR LEAD.*

BABBITT METAL.

SQUARE CAKE   AND   J. B.

SOLDER.

PIGS.   CAKES.   BARS.

Floating and Capping.

SPELTER.

LEHIGH   AND   SILESIAN.

ZINC NAILS.

$\frac{3}{4}$, 1, $1\frac{1}{8}$ and $1\frac{1}{4}$ inches.

SPELTER OR BRAZIER'S SOLDER.

FINE AND COARSE.

AGENTS FOR THE SALE OF

Patent Lead Pipe, Sheet Lead, etc.,

MANUFACTURED BY

TATHAM & BROTHERS,

WATER PIPES FOR HYDRANTS, PUMPS, &c.

Calibre of Pipe.	Weight per Rod and Foot.	Average Length of Coils.	Calibre of Pipe.	Weight per Rod and Foot.	Average Length of Coils.	Calibre of Pipe.	Weight per Rod and Foot.	Average Length of Coils.
Ins.		Feet.	Ins.		Feet.	Ins.		Feet.
⅜	7 lb. per rod.		¾	2½ lb. per ft.	75	2	4¾ lb. per ft.	30
⅜	10 oz. per ft.	100	¾	3 lb. "	65	2	6 lb. "	45
⅜	1 lb. "	75	¾	3½ lb. "	60	2	7 lb. "	40
⅜	1¼ lb. "	75	1	24¾ lb. per rod.		2	9 lb. "	30
⅜	1½ lb. "	150	1	2 lb. per ft.	60	2½	8 lb. "	35
½	9 lb. per rod.	150	1	2½ lb. "	75	2½	11 lb. "	30
½	¾ lb. per ft.	100	1	3¼ lb. "	60	2½	14 lb. "	20
½	1 lb. "	100	1	4 lb. "	50	2½	17 lb. "	18
½	1¼ lb. "	100	1	4¾ lb. "	45	3	9 lb. "	20
½	1¾ lb. "	100	1¼	2 lb. "	60	3	12 lb. "	20
½	2 lb. "	100	1¼	2½ ib. "	50	3	16 lb. "	20
½	2½ lb. "	85	1¼	3 lb. "	65	3	20 lb. "	16
½	3 lb. "	70	1¼	3¾ lb. "	50	3½	12½ lb. "	20
⅝	14 lb. per rod.		1¼	4¾ lb. "	42	3½	15 lb. "	20
⅝	1 lb. per ft.	125	1¼	6 lb. "	36	3½	18½ lb. "	18
⅝	1½ lb. "	100	1½	3½ lb. "	35	3½	22 lb. "	13
⅝	2 lb. "	100	1½	4¼ lb. "	30	4	12 lb. "	18
⅝	2½ lb. "	95	1½	5 lb. "	22	4	16 lb. "	15
⅝	2¾ lb. "	85	1½	6½ lb. "	28	4	21 lb. "	12
⅝	3 lb. "	70	1½	8 lb. "	23	4	25 lb. "	15
⅝	3½ lb. "	60	1¾	4 lb. "	25	4½	14 lb. "	18
¾	16 lb. per rod.		1¾	5 lb. "	22	4½	18 lb. "	10
¾	1½ lb. per ft.	80	1¾	6½ lb. "	28	5	20 lb. "	9
¾	2 lb. "	95	1¾	8½ lb. "	22	5	31 lb. "	7

WASTE PIPE.

1½ inch, 2 lb. per foot.
2 " 3 lb. "
3 " 3½ and 5 lb. per foot.

4 inch, 5, 6 and 8 lb. per foot.
4½ " 6 and 8 lb. "
5 " 8, 10 and 12 lb. "

BLOCK-TIN PIPE.

⅜ inch, 4¾, 6 and 8 oz. per foot.
½ " 6, 8 and 10 oz. "
⅝ " 8 and 10 oz. "
¾ " 10 and 12 oz. "

1 inch, 15 and 18 oz. per foot.
1¼ " 1¼ and 1½ lb. "
1½ " 2 and 2½ lb. "
2 " 3 lb. "

MINERAL-WATER PIPE.

LEAD PIPE.

3-16 inch. ¼ inch. ⅜ inch.

COMPOSITION.

3-16 inch. ¼ inch. ⅜ inch.

SHEET LEAD.

Weight of square foot, 2½, 3, 3½, 4, 4½, 5, 6, 7, 8, 9, 10 lbs. and upwards.

E. L. PARKER & CO., BALTIMORE.

WROUGHT IRON AND GALVANIZED PIPE,

Malleable and Cast Iron Fittings

FOR GAS, STEAM AND WATER,

GAS AND STEAM FITTERS' TOOLS, &c.

IRON PIPE.	1/8	1/4	3/8	1/2	3/4	1	1 1/4	1 1/2	2	2 1/2	3	3 1/2	4	4 1/2	5	6
Wrought Iron Pipe, per ft.	07	08	10	12	15	22	30	38	56	90	1 30	1 60	2 06	2 40	2 80	4 00
Galvanized Pipe, designed especially for water,	....	....	16	18	24	34	44	56	75	1 30	1 65	....	....	....	....	....

FITTINGS FOR WROUGHT IRON TUBE.

Nominal Diam., inches.	1/8	1/4	3/8	1/2	3/4	1	1 1/4	1 1/2	2	2 1/2	3	3 1/2	4	4 1/2	5	6
Longscrews	....	25	30	35	44	62	88	1 15	1 80	2 90	4 40	5 75	....	....	....	....
Couplings, Plugs, Lock Nuts	07	08	09	10	14	19	26	35	57	95	1 35	2 15	2 50	3 30	4 15	5 95
Reducing Sockets, Right and Left Hand Sockets, Caps, Bushings	09	10	11	12	16	23	32	42	69	1 16	1 64	2 61	3 03	3 93	5 06	7 20
Close Nipples, Shoulder Nipples	07	08	09	10	14	19	26	35	57	95	1 35	2 15	2 50	....	....	....
Cutting Off and Cutting Threads	06	07	08	10	12	18	25	32	46	85	1 25	1 60	2 00	....	....	....
Crosses	18	20	22	26	36	49	67	89	1 46	2 50	3 50	4 90	6 40	8 50	10 70	15 30
Tees	14	15	17	20	28	38	52	69	1 13	1 90	2 70	3 80	5 00	6 60	8 30	11 90
Drop Tees	....	....	....	30	37	49	....	....	....	....	....	....	....	....	....	....
Elbows	10	11	12	14	20	27	37	49	81	1 30	1 90	2 70	3 60	4 70	5 90	8 50
Drop Elbows	....	....	....	24	28	38	....	....	....	....	....	....	....	....	....	....
Return Bends, close pat'n.	....	....	15	20	28	44	62	88	1 25	1 90	....	....	....	....	....	....
Return Bends, wide pat'n.	....	....	18	24	33	53	74	1 06	1 50	2 30	....	....	....	....	....	....
Unions	....	40	50	60	80	1 00	1 30	1 60	2 40	3 40	4 75	6 40	....	....	....	....
Wrought Iron Bends	....	22	25	30	38	50	69	88	1 31	....	....	....	....	....	....	....

GALVANIZED FITTINGS FOR WROUGHT IRON TUBES.

Nominal Diameter, inches.	1/4	3/8	1/2	3/4	1	1 1/4	1 1/2	2	2 1/2	3
Long Screws	29	35	41	52	75	1 06	1 40	2 10	3 40	5 25
Sockets, Plugs, Lock Nuts	08	09	11	16	23	35	45	70	1 15	1 70
Reducing Sockets, Right and Left Sockets, Caps and Wrought Lock Nuts	10	12	14	20	28	40	53	85	1 45	2 10
Nipples	12	14	16	24	36	50	63	1 00	1 65	2 50
Crosses	22	24	28	41	59	86	1 12	1 80	3 00	4 45
Tees	17	18	22	32	46	67	87	1 40	2 35	3 45
Elbows	12	13	16	23	33	48	62	1 00	1 68	2 45
Return Bends	....	....	25	31	55	76	1 07	1 62	....	....

TINNERS'
FURNISHING
SUPPLIES.

E. L. PARKER & CO., BALTIMORE.

AGENTS FOR THE SALE OF

PLYMOUTH RIVETS,

Warranted the Best now in use.

IRON—Tinned.

8 oz.	. .	48 cents per M.	2 lbs.	. .	1 00 cents per M.
10 oz.	. .	52 " "	2½ lbs.	. .	1 20 " "
12 oz.	. .	56 " "	3 lbs.	. .	1 45 " "
1 lb.	. .	63 " "	4 lbs.	. .	1 75 " "
1¼ lbs.	. .	70 " "	5 lbs.	. .	2 05 " "
1½ lbs.	. .	80 " "	6 lbs.	. .	2 40 " "
1¾ lbs.	. .	90 " "	7 lbs.	. .	2 75 " "

IRON—Black.

8 oz.	. .	40 cents per M.	4 lbs.	. .	1 30 cents per M.
10 oz.	. .	45 " "	5 lbs.	. .	1 50 " "
12 oz.	. .	50 " "	6 lbs.	. .	1 75 " "
1 lb.	. .	55 " "	7 lbs.	. .	2 00 " "
1¼ lbs.	. .	60 " "	8 lbs.	. .	2 20 " "
1½ lbs.	. .	66 " "	9 lbs.	. .	2 45 " "
1¾ lbs.	. .	73 " "	10 lbs.	. .	2 70 " "
2 lbs.	. .	80 " "	12 lbs.	. .	3 15 " "
2½ lbs.	. .	95 " "	14 lbs.	. .	3 60 " "
3 lbs.	. .	1 15 " "			

BLOCK AND CARRIAGE RIVETS.

100 RIVETS EACH.

W. G.	¾	⅞	1	1⅛	1¼	1½	1¾	2	2¼	2½	3	3½	4 Inches.
3	48	52	56	63	75	88	1 00	1 12	1 25	1 45	1 60	1 90	2 25
4	44	48	52	56	65	75	88	1 00	1 12	1 25	1 45	1 75	1 90
5	38	42	45	50	56	73	82	90	1 00	1 12	1 25	1 45	1 75
6	32	36	40	46	52	60	70	80	90	1 00	1 20	1 40	1 60
7	30	33	36	40	45	50	56	62	70	80	95	1 12	1 25
8	22	25	28	32	38	44	50	56	65	75	88	1 00	1 15

RIVETS IN KEGS.

OF 100 POUNDS EACH.

	Per lb.		Per lb.
3 lb. Black	. . .	7 lb. Black	. . .
4 " "	. . .	8 " "	. . .
5 " "	. . .	9 " "	. . .
6 " "	. . .	10 " "	. . .

COOPERS' RIVETS IN KEGS.

OF 100 POUNDS EACH.

	Per lb.		Per lb.
3 Penny,	. . .	5 Penny,	. . .
4 "	. . .	6 "	. . .

Oval or Countersunk Heads or Extra Lengths, 5 cents per M. extra.
Coopers' Rivets, from one to six penny, in papers of 10 lbs. each.
Safe, Tank and Hoe Rivets made to order, of any size not to exceed ⅜ inch wire.
Tinned Hose and Belt Rivets and Burrs, all sizes.

Copper Hose and Belt Rivets and Burrs, all sizes.

COPPERSMITHS' RIVETS.

Nos. 1, 2, 3, 4, 5 and 6.

TINNED AND BLOCK BURRS.

Nos. 6, 7, 8 and 9.

STOVE BOLTS.

1-4 Inch.		5-16 Inch.	
Length.	Per 100	Length.	Per 100
¾ inch,	. . . .	¾ inch,	. . . .
1 "	. . . .	1 "	. . . .
1¼ "	. . . .	1¼ "	. . . .
1½ "	. . . .	1½ "	. . . .
1¾ "	. . . .	1¾ "	. . . .
2 "	. . . .	2 "	. . . .
2¼ "	. . . .	2¼ "	. . . .
2½ "	. . . .	2½ "	. . . .
2¾ "	. . . .	2¾ "	. . . .
3 "	. . . .	3 "	. . . .

KETTLE EARS.

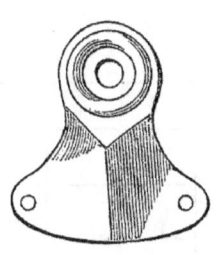 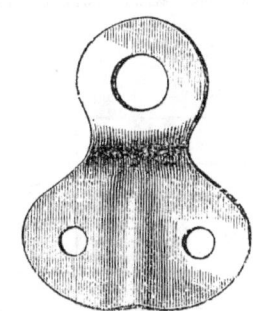 

TIN AND TINNED IRON.

No.	1	2	3	4	5	6	7	8
Per gross pairs,	88	1 00	1 50	1 75	2 10	2 75	3 75	4 50

IRON, BLACK.

No.	1	2	3	4	5	6	7	8
Per gross pairs,	75	88	1 35	1 50	1 75	2 25	3 25	4 00

TINNED SAUCE-PAN HANDLES.

MALLEABLE IRON.

5, 6, 7 Inch. 8, 9 Inch.

No.	1	2	3	4	5	6	7	8
Inches,	4½	5	6	7	8	9	10	11
Per gross,								
Per dozen,								

FRENCH SAUCE-PAN HANDLES.

TINNED.

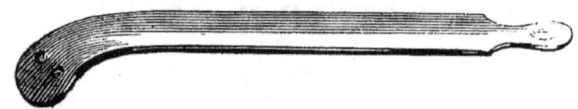

No.	1	2	3	4	5	6
Inches,	6	7	8	9	10	11
Per gross,						
Per dozen,						

FORGED SAUCE-PAN HANDLES.

BLACK.

No.	1	2	3	4	5
Inches,	5	6	7	8	9
Per gross,					
Per dozen,					

E. L. PARKER & CO., BALTIMORE.

BRASS KETTLES.

SCALE OF SIZES, WEIGHT AND CAPACITY.

Diameter.	Weight.	Capacity.	Diameter.	Weight.	Capacity.
7 inch,	1 pound,	½ gal.	16 inch,	7½ pound,	6 gal.
8 "	1½ "	1 "	17 "	9 "	8 "
9 "	2½ "	1½ "	18 "	10½ "	10 "
10 "	3 "	2 "	19 "	12½ "	12 "
11 "	3½ "	2½ "	20 "	16½ "	14 "
12 "	4 "	3 "	22 "	20 "	18 "
13 "	5 "	4 "	24 "	27½ "	25 "
14 "	5¾ "	4½ "	26 "	34½ "	32 "
15 "	6½ "	5 "			

COPPER KETTLES.

8, 9, 10, 11, 12, 13, 14, 15, 16, 17, 18, 19, 20, 22, 24, 26 inch.

Same weight and capacity as the brass.

Brass Wash Basins, ... per pound
Brass Dippers, ... "
Copper Dippers, ... "

TIN TIPPED TEA POT HANDLE.

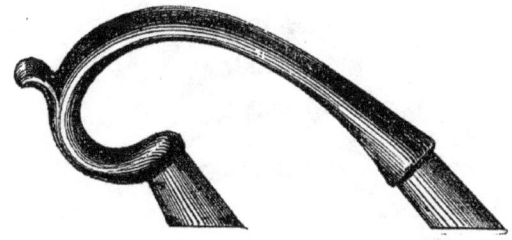

No. 10, Small, .   No. 15, Medium, .   No. 20, Large, .

The very general use of these made by tinners throughout the country, has induced extra pains in their manufacture. The tin tips are securely fastened, and are so made that they must necessarily fit without the use of shears. We only ask a trial to convince the trade they are the best in market.

PATENT HOLLOW TIN AND IRON TEA POT HANDLE.

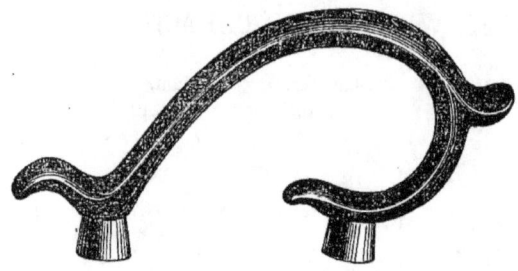

These handles are made of iron and tin, and are hollow, allowing a free circulation of air through them, which prevents their becoming heated.

	Per gross.	Per doz.		Per gross.	Per doz.
No. 1, Black, small,			No. 100, White,		
2, " med.			115, "		
3, " large,			210, Black,		
			215, "		

TEA AND COFFEE POT SPOUTS.

	Per gross.	Per dozen.
No. 1, Tea Pot, small,		
2, " " med.		
3, Coffee Pot, large		

CAN SPOUTS.

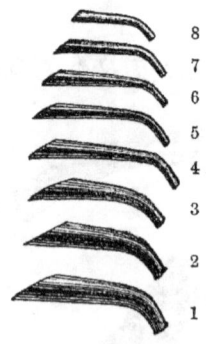

No.		1	2	3	4	5	6	7	8
Length,	in.	$6\frac{3}{4}$	$6\frac{1}{2}$	$5\frac{3}{4}$	$6\frac{1}{4}$	6	$5\frac{3}{4}$	$5\frac{1}{2}$	$3\frac{3}{4}$
Per gross,									
Per dozen,									

Patent Metallic Wash Boiler Bottoms.

PLAIN AND CORRUGATED.

This bottom will resist the action of acids and alkalies, and does not corrode at the seam.

Size of hole in stove,	in.	5	5½	6	7	8	9	10
Length of bottom,	in.	13	13¼	14	15¾	17½	19	22
Depth,	in.	1	1	1	1	1	1	1
Width of flanges,	in.	1¾—2½	1¾—2½	1¾—2½	1¾—2½	1¾—2½	1¾—2½	1¾—2½
Per pound,								

Patent Metallic Square Flange Bottoms.

DOUBLE PITS.

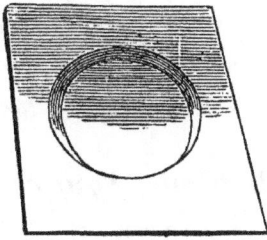

Size of hole in stove,	in.	5	5½	6	7	8	9	10
Depth,	in.	1	1	1	1	1	1	1
Width of flanges,	in.	2¼—2½	2¼—2½	2¼—2½	2¼—2½	2¼—2½	2¼—2½	2¼—2½
Per pound,								

Patent Metallic Round Tea Kettle Bottoms.

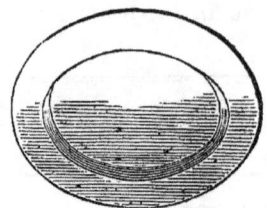

Size of hole in stove,	in.	5	5½	6	7	8	9	10
Width of flanges,	in.	1½	1½	1½	1½	1¾	1¾	1¾
Depth,	in.	1	1	1	1	1	1	1
Per pound,								

Copper Wash Boiler Bottoms.
OVAL.

Size of hole in stove,	in.	5	5½	6	7	8	9	10
Length of bottom,	in.	13	13¼	14	16	17½	19½	22
Depth,	in.	1⅛	1⅛	1⅛	1⅛	1⅛	1⅛	1⅛
Width of flanges,	in.	2—3¾	2—2¾	2—2¾	2—2¾	2—2¾	2—2¾	2—2¾
Per pound,								

Copper Bottoms, Square Flange.
DOUBLE PIT.

Size of hole in stove,	in.	5	5½	6	7	8	9	10
Depth,	in.	1⅛	1⅛	1⅛	1⅛	1⅛	1⅛	1⅛
Width of flanges,	in.	2—2¼	2—2¼	2—2¼	2—2¼	2—2¼	2—2¼	2—2¼
Per pound,								

Copper Bottoms.—Round Tea Kettle Bottoms.

Size of hole in stove, . .	in.	5	$5\frac{1}{2}$	6	7	8	9	10
Depth, ...	in.	$1\frac{1}{8}$	$1\frac{1}{8}$	$1\frac{1}{8}$	$1\frac{1}{8}$	$1\frac{1}{8}$	$1\frac{1}{8}$	$1\frac{1}{8}$
Width of flanges, . . .	in.	$1\frac{1}{4}$	$1\frac{1}{4}$	$1\frac{1}{4}$	$1\frac{1}{4}$	$1\frac{1}{4}$	$1\frac{1}{4}$	$1\frac{1}{4}$
Per pound, ...								

Wash Boiler Cover or Top.

STAMPED TIN.

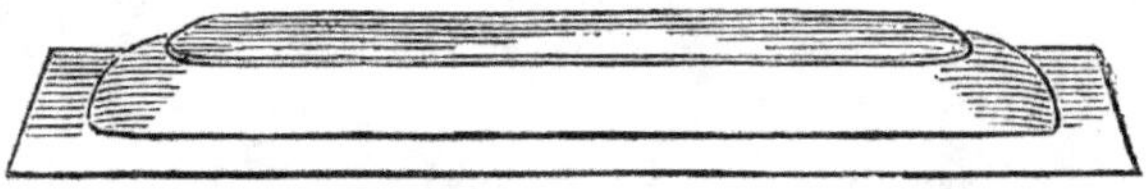

This forms a neat and economical top to a wash boiler, and supersedes those made by hand.

Size of boiler bottom, . .	in.	$5\frac{1}{2}$	6	7	8	9	10
Size of top to suit the bottom,	in.	$9\frac{1}{2}$x18	10x$19\frac{1}{4}$	$10\frac{1}{2}$x21	$11\frac{3}{4}$x$22\frac{1}{4}$	$12\frac{3}{4}$x$24\frac{1}{4}$	$13\frac{1}{2}$x$25\frac{1}{2}$
Per dozen, ...							

"IMPROVED"
Wash Boiler Cover or Top.

STAMPED TIN.

Size of boiler bottom, . .	in.	$5\frac{1}{2}$	6	7	8	9	10
Size of top to suit the bottom,	in.		$9\frac{1}{8}$x$17\frac{7}{8}$	$9\frac{5}{8}$x$19\frac{1}{4}$	$10\frac{5}{8}$x$20\frac{1}{4}$	$12\frac{1}{8}$x$22\frac{1}{2}$	
Per dozen, ...							

This cover has the edges turned so as to fit on the wire rim running around the boiler, making an easy fit and a neat boiler top. The measure given here is the exact size of the top.

PLAIN AND TINNED
MALLEABLE IRON CASTINGS.

Malleable Iron Handles,
FOR WATER COOLERS, TOILET WARE, ETC., ETC.

1 2 3   *4*   *5*

 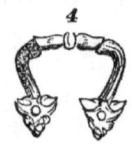 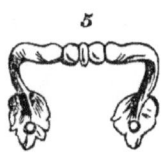

Plain, ... per lb.   Tinned, ... per lb.

Grey Iron Handles,
FOR WATER COOLERS, TOILET WARE, ETC., DRILLED.

1   *2*   *4*

3

Plain, ... per lb.
Common, ... "

Stove Pipe Dampers.

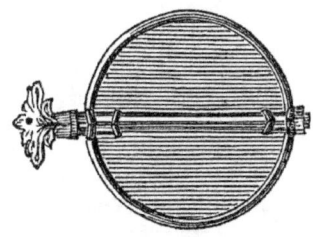

Inches, ...	4	4½	5	5½	6	7
Per pound, ...						

Stove Catches.

Nos. 1 2 3   4

Plain, ... per lb.

Stove Hinges.

No. 1   2

Plain, ... per lb.

Stove Turnbuckles.

Nos. 1   2   3   4   5   6   7

Round Shank.
    Round Shank.

Plain, ... per lb.

Stove Turnbuckle Tongues.

1   2

Plain, ... per lb.

Coal Hod Handles and Ears.

Plain, ... per lb.

Iron Kettle Ears.

0

3

PLAIN.					TINNED.				
Nos...	1	2	3	4	Nos...	1	2	3	4
Per pound, .					Per pound,				

Stove Knobs.
JAPANNED.

No. 1, Plain, ... per lb.
   2,   "   . . . .   "

Shovel Shanks.

Plain, ... per lb.

Wood Bucket Ears.

Plain, ... per lb.

Tureen or Butter Kettle Lid Handles.
MALLEABLE IRON.
Nos. 1 2 3

Plain, ... per lb.
Tinned, ...   "

Milk Can Handles.
GREY IRON.

No. 1   2

No. 1, Plain, . . . per lb.
   2,   "   . . .   "
No. 1, Tinned, . .   "
   2,   "   . .   "

Stove Drawer Handles.

Plain, ... per lb.

Tureen Feet.
MALLEABLE IRON.

Plain, ... per lb.
Tinned, ...   "

E. L. PARKER & CO., BALTIMORE.

STOVE ORNAMENTS.

No.	Per dozen.	No.	Per dozen.
1	. . . . .	43	. . . . .
2	. . . . .	44	. . . . .
3	. . . . .	45	. . . . .
5	. . . . .	46	. . . . .
6	. . . . .	47	. . . . .
7	. . . . .	48	. . . . .
8	. . . . .	49	. . . . .
10	. . . . .	50	. . . . .
11	. . . . .	51	. . . . .
12	. . . . .	52	. . . . .
14	. . . . .	53	. . . . .
15	. . . . .	54	. . . . .
16	. . . . .	55	. . . . .
18	. . . . .	56	. . . . .
20	. . . . .	57	. . . . .
21	. . . . .	58	. . . . .
22	. . . . .	59	. . . . .
23	. . . . .	60	. . . . .
24	. . . . .	61	. . . . .
27	. . . . .	62	. . . . .
29	. . . . .	63	. . . . .
31	. . . . .	64	. . . . .
32	. . . . .	65	. . . . .
34	. . . . .	66	. . . . .
35	. . . . .	67	. . . . .
38	. . . . .	68	. . . . .
40	. . . . .	69	. . . . .
41	. . . . .	70	. . . . .
42	. . . . .		

MICA OR ISINGLASS.

Per pound,	$	$	$	$	$
2 in.	2 x 3 2 3½ 2 4 2 4½ 2 5	2 x 5½ 2 6 2 6½ 2 7 2 7½	2 x 8 2 8½	2 x 9 2 9½	2 x 10
2½ in.	2½ x 3 2½ 3½ 2½ 4 2½ 4½	2½ x 5 2½ 5½ 2½ 6 2½ 6½	2½ x 7 2½ 7½	2½ x 8 2½ 8½ 2½ 9 2½ 9½	2½ x 10 and upwards.
3 in.	3 x 3 3 3½ 3 4 3 4½	3 x 5 3 5½	3 x 6 3 6½ 3 7 3 7½	3 x 8 3 8½ 3 9	3 x 9½
3½ in.	3½ x 3½ 3½ 4	3½ x 4½ 3½ 5 3½ 5½	3½ x 6 3½ 6½ 3½ 7 3½ 7½	3½ x 8 3½ 8½ 3½ 9	3½ x 9½ and upwards.
4 in.		4 x 4 4 4½	4 x 5 4 5½ 4 6 4 6½	4 x 7 4 7½ 4 8 4 8½	4 x 9
4½ in.			4½ x 4½ 4½ 5 4½ 5½ 4½ 6	4½ x 6½ 4½ 7 4½ 7½ 4½ 8 4½ 8½	4½ x 9
5 in.			5 x 5 5 5½ 5 6 5 6½	5 x 7 5 7½ 5 8 5 8½	5 x 9
5½ in.			5½ x 5½ 5½ 6 5½ 6½	5½ x 7 5½ 7½ 5½ 8 5½ 8½	5½ x 9
6 in.			6 x 6 6 6½	6 x 7 6 7½ 6 8 6 8½	6 x 9 and upwards. " " " " " "
7 in.				7 x 7 7 7½	7 x 8 and upwards. " "
8 to 12 in.					8 x 8 and upwards. 9 9 " 10 10 " 11 11 " 12 12 "

BRASS WIRE CLOTH.—For Strainers.

IN 5 FOOT ROLLS.

	Per roll.	Per foot.
Fine,		
Medium,		
Coarse,		

"BRASS" EXTINGUISHERS.

	Per gross.
Brass Fluid,	
Tubed Chained, No. 1,	
" " 2,	
Can Spout,	

SOLDERING COPPERS.

	Per lb.
All sizes,	

CORRUGATED FUNNEL TUBES.

No.		1	2	3	4	5
Calibre,	in.	$\frac{1}{4}$	$\frac{3}{8}$	$\frac{1}{2}$	$\frac{5}{8}$	$\frac{3}{4}$
Per gross,						
Per dozen,						

GRATER BLANK.

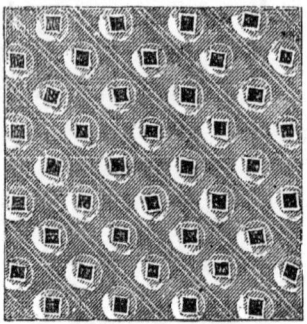

Sheet, . . .	$\frac{1}{4}$	$\frac{1}{2}$	1
Per gross, . .			
Per dozen, . .			

The exact texture, size of holes, and distances between them, is shown in the cut.

SCREW TOPS FOR OIL AND FLUID CANS.

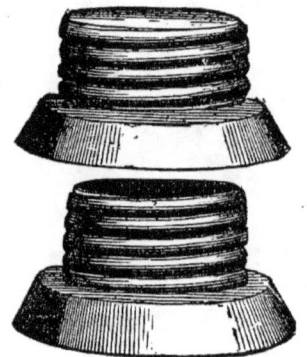

ZINC.

Inches, ...	$\frac{1}{2}$	$\frac{3}{4}$	1	$1\frac{1}{4}$	$1\frac{1}{2}$
Per gross, ...					
Per dozen, ...					

BRASS.

Inches, ...	$\frac{1}{2}$	$\frac{3}{4}$	1	$1\frac{1}{4}$	$1\frac{1}{2}$
Per gross, ...					
Per dozen, ...					

TEA OR COFFEE POT KNOBS.

Per gross. Per dozen. Per gross. Per dozen.

Bird, Bright, ...

1 X, Bright, ...

2 X, Bright, ...

Acorn, Bright, . . .

3 X, Bright, ...

No. 1, Oval, Black, .

No. 100, Round, Black,
200,   "   "
300,   "   "
100,   "   Bright,
200,   "   "
300,   "   "

No. 2, Oval, Black, .
No. 3,   "   "   .

1 X, Black, ...

No. 175, ...
180, ...
190, ...
195, ...

2 X, Black, ...

Tin Knobs, No. 1, . .
"   "   " 2, . .
"   "   " 3, . .

3 X, Black, ...

PERFORATED TIN.

No. 1   2   3

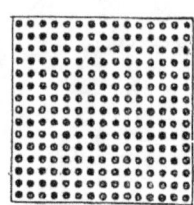 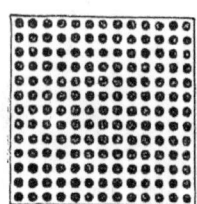

Per dozen. Per sheet.

Fine, No. 1, 10x14, ...
Medium, No. 2, 10x14, ...
Coarse, No. 3, 10x14, ...

These cuts of perforated tin represent the exact texture, size of holes, and distances between them.

ZINC, BRASS AND TIN OILERS.

 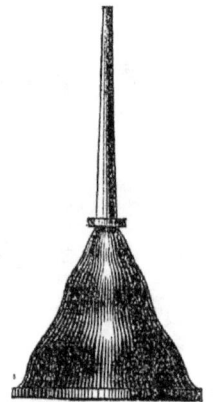 

Per gross. Per dozen. Per gross. Per dozen.

No. 0, Zinc,	.	.	No. 0, Brass,	.
1, "	.	.	1, "	.
2, "	.	.	2, "	.
3, "	.	.	3, "	.
4, "	.	.	4, "	.
5, "	.	.	5, "	.
Long Tube, extra,	.		Long Tube, extra,	.
" " bent extra,			" " bent extra,	
Short " "	.		Short " "	
No. 1, Tin,	.	.		
2, "	.	.		
3, "	.	.		

FIRE POTS.

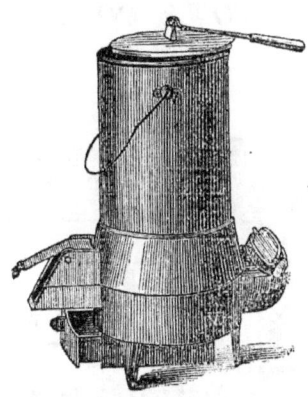

Price.

Improved Base Burning,
No. 1, Large with grate,
    2, Small, "
    1, Large, no grate,
    2, Small, "

ROSIN.

Per lb.

No. 1, Best,
    2, "
    3, "

WOODEN WARE.

Mallets.   *Bucket Handles.*

Soldering Iron Handles.   *Hammer Handles.*

Rolling Pins.   *Mashers.*

STOVE POLISH.

Per gross. Per dozen.

ARROW POLISH, ...
MORRILL'S, ...
DIXON'S, ...

BLACK LEAD IN BULK.

Per lb.

BEST No. 1, LUMP, ...
" 2, " . . . .
" 3, " . . . .

STAMPED AND PLAIN TIN WARE,

House Furnishing Goods,

&c., &c.

POT COVERS.

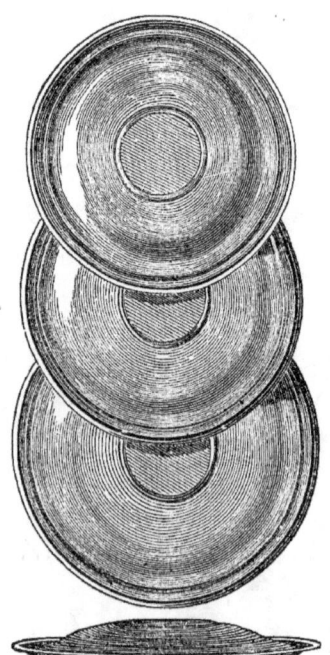

Inches,	7	7¼	7½	7¾	8	8¼	8½
Per gross,							
Per dozen,							
Inches,	8¾	9	9¼	9½	9¾	10	10¼
Per gross,							
Per dozen,							
Inches,	10½	10¾	11	11¼	11½	11¾	12
Per gross,							
Per dozen,							
Inches,	12¼	12½	12¾	13	13¼	13½	13¾
Per gross,							
Per dozen,							

Measure from outside edges.

STEAMER BOTTOMS.

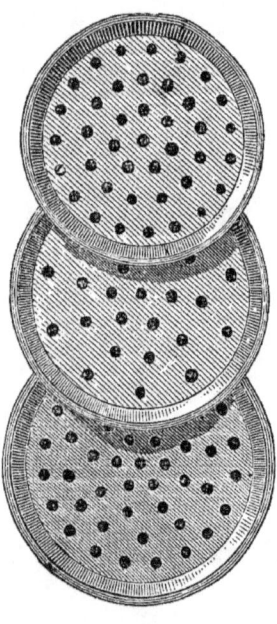

Inches,	7	7¼	7½	7¾	8	8¼	8½
Per gross,							
Per dozen,							
Inches,	8¾	9	9¼	9½	9¾	10	10¼
Per gross,							
Per dozen,							
Inches,	10½	10¾	11	11¼	11½	11¾	12
Per gross,							
Per dozen,							
Inches,	12¼	12½	12¾	13	13¼	13½	13¾
Per gross,							
Per dozen,							

Outside measure.

BUCKET OR PAIL COVERS.

OUTSIDE MEASURE.

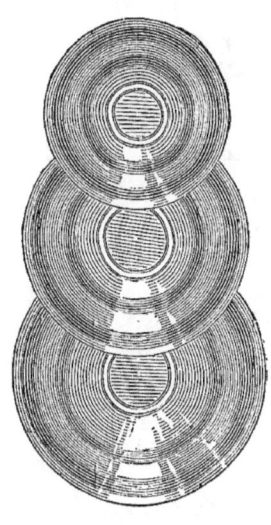

Inches,	$4\tfrac{1}{2}$	$5\tfrac{3}{8}$	$6\tfrac{1}{4}$	$6\tfrac{7}{8}$	$7\tfrac{5}{8}$	$8\tfrac{1}{2}$
Quarts,	$\tfrac{1}{2}$	1	2	3	4	6
Per gross,						
Per dozen,						
Inches,	$9\tfrac{1}{8}$	$9\tfrac{1}{2}$	$10\tfrac{1}{2}$	11	$11\tfrac{1}{2}$	
Quarts,	8	10	12	14	16	
Per gross,						
Per dozen,						

Plain Coffee Pot Tops.
EDGES FLAT.

Per gross. Per dozen.

2 pints, $3\tfrac{1}{8}$ inches, .
2 quarts, $3\tfrac{3}{8}$ " .
3 " $3\tfrac{3}{4}$ " .
4 " $4\tfrac{1}{2}$ " .
5 " $5\tfrac{1}{8}$ " .
6 " $5\tfrac{3}{4}$ " .

Round Tea Pot Tops.
RE-TINNED.

Per gross. Per dozen.

2 pints, $4\tfrac{3}{8}$ inches, .
3 " $4\tfrac{3}{4}$ " .
4 " $5\tfrac{1}{4}$ " .
5 " $5\tfrac{1}{2}$ " .
6 " 6 " .

Round Tea Pot Tops.
EDGES TURNED.   HINGED.

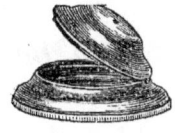

Per gross. Per dozen.

2 pints, $3\tfrac{3}{4}$ inches, .
3 " $4\tfrac{1}{8}$ " .
4 " $4\tfrac{3}{8}$ " .
5 " $4\tfrac{7}{8}$ " .
6 " $5\tfrac{1}{4}$ " .

Wash Bowl Bottoms.
PLAIN.

Per gross. Per dozen.

$5\tfrac{3}{4}$ inches, ...
$6\tfrac{1}{4}$ " . . . .
$6\tfrac{1}{2}$ " . . . .

ROUND
Spun Tea Pot Tops.
EDGES TURNED.

Oval Tea Pot Tops.
RE-TINNED. HINGED.

Per gross. Per dozen.

Per gross. Per dozen.

2 pints, 3¾ inches, .
3 "   4⅕   "   .
4 "   4⅜   "   .
5 "   4⅞   "   .
6 "   5¼   "   .

2 pints, 3¾x5⅜ in. .
3 "   4¼x5¾ " .
4 "   4¾x6¼ " .
5 "   5¼x6⅝ " .
6 "   5¾x7⅛ " .

ROUND
Tin Tea Kettle or Coffee Boiler Bottoms.

Sink, ...	in.	5	5½	6	7	8	9
Flanges, ...	in.	1¼	1¼	1¼	1¼	1¼	1¼
Per gross, ...							
Per dozen, ...							

ROUND
Tin Bottoms with Square Flange.

Sink, ...	in.	6	7	8	9
Flange, ...	in.	2½x2	2½x2	3x2½	3x2½
Per gross, ...					
Per dozen, ...					

CANDLESTICK BOTTOMS.

Per gross. Per dozen.

No. 1, ...
   2, ...
   3, ...
No. 1, deep, ...
   2, " . . . .
Candlestick Tops, ...
   " Braces, ...
   " Springs, common, ...
   " Springs, screw, ...

TEA KETTLES.—Breasts and Covers.

OUTSIDE MEASURE.

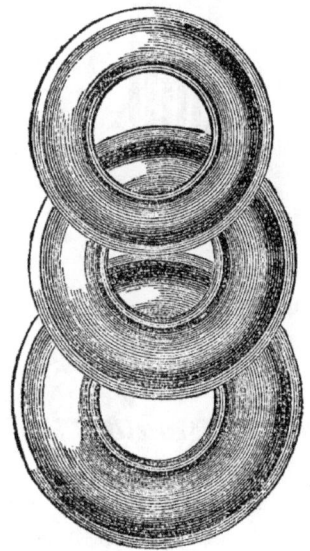

Inches, . . .	$5\frac{1}{2}$	6	$6\frac{1}{2}$	7	$7\frac{1}{2}$	8
Per gross, . . .						
Per dozen, . .						
Inches, . . .	$8\frac{1}{2}$	9	$9\frac{1}{2}$	10	$10\frac{1}{2}$	11
Per gross, . . .						
Per dozen, . . .						
Inches, . . .	$11\frac{1}{2}$	12	$12\frac{1}{2}$	13	$13\frac{1}{2}$	14
Per gross, . . .						
Per dozen, . . .						

Tureen or Butter Kettle Covers.

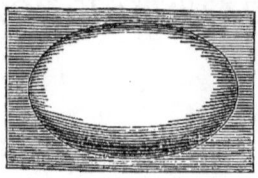

	Per gross.	Per dozen.
Square, No. 1, 6½x10 inches, P		
" " 2,		
" " 3, 6½x10 inches,		
" " 3½, 6½x10 inches,		
" " 4,		
" " 5, 8x12 inches,		
Oval Deep, No. 1, small, 8x10¾ inches,		
" " 2, medium, 8¾x11¼ inches,		
" " 3, large, 9x11¾ inches,		

Fluid Cans.

Per dozen.

1 Pint,	
1 Quart,	
2 "	
4 "	

Candle Mould Pans.

	Per gross.	Per dozen.
3 Hole,		
4 "		
6 "		
8 "		
10 "		
12 "		

Candle Moulds.

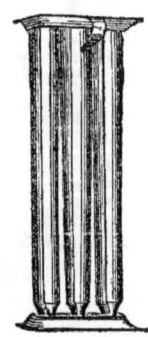

	Per gross.	Per dozen.
3 Hole,		
4 "		
6 "		
8 "		
10 "		
12 "		

Candle Mould Tips.

	Per gross.	Per dozen
No. 1,		

SLOP PAIL FIXTURES.

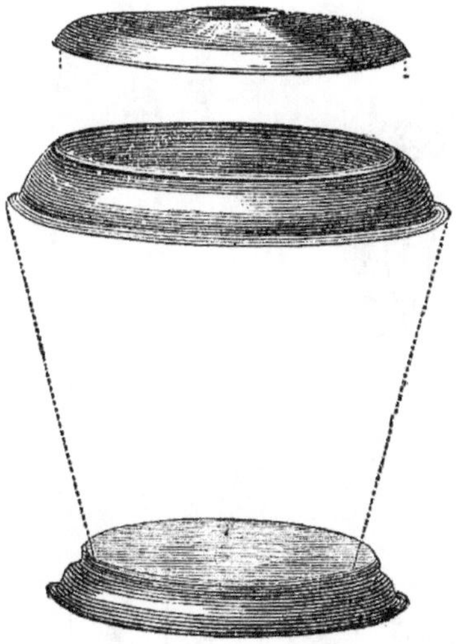

BREAST, COVER, FOOT.

Sets, ...	*No.*	*100*	*250*	*350*
Diam. Breast, . .	in.	12⅜	11¾	10
Diam. Foot, . .	in.	8¼	7¾	6⅜
Diam. Cover, . .	in.	10	9	8
Per gross, . . .				
Per dozen, . . .				

These fixtures constitute nearly all, and the most difficult part of the work in a chamber pail; with these, apprentices or ordinary workmen can manufacture pails rapidly and economically.

TOILET JAR FIXTURES.

FLUTED COVERS.

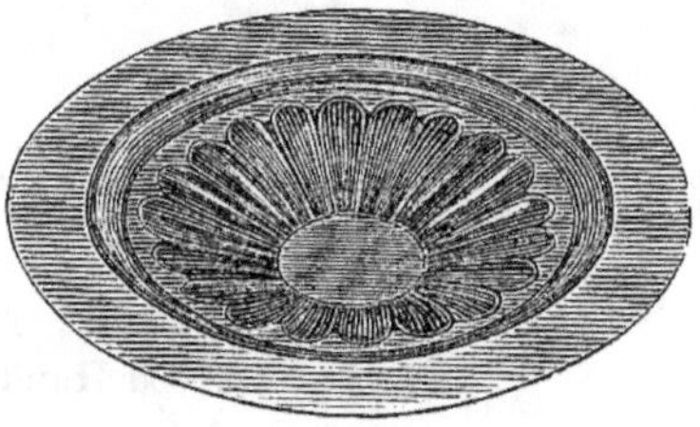

	Per gross.	Per dozen.
Fluted Covers, 10½ inches, ...		
Bottom or Foot, 7½ inches across top, ...		
Cesspools, 3⅝ inches, ...		
Sets, ...		

STAMPED PIPE RINGS.

SIZE OF HOLE.

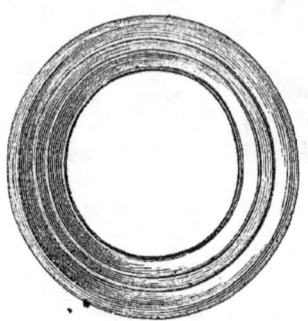

ZINC OR TIN.

Inches,	4	4½	5	5½	6	7	8
Per gross,							
Per dozen,							

Fruit Can Tops and Bottoms.

              Per gross. Per dozen.

1 Qt., Top alone, . .
1 " Bottom " . .
1 " Tops & Bottoms,

Can Wax.

Per pound, ...

Tea Pot Hinges.

            Per gross. Per dozen.

No. 1, ...
    2, ...
    3, ...

Ice Picks.

            Per gross. Per dozen.

Iron, ...
Wood Handle, . .

Pan Studs.

Brass and Copper Dipper Bowls.

PIE PLATES.

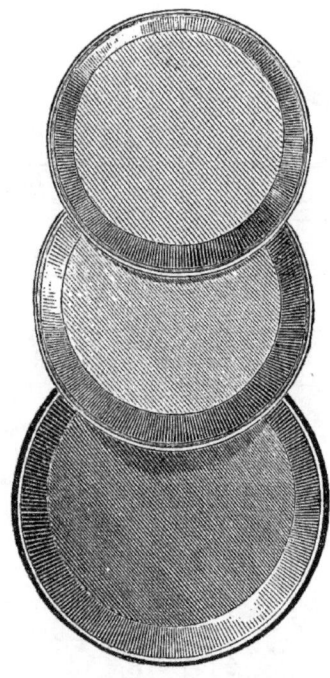

Inches,	6	7	8	9	10
Per gross,					
Per dozen,					

EXTRA DEEP.

Inches,	8	9	10
Per gross,			
Per dozen,			

DINING PLATES.

Inches,	6	7	8	9	10
Per gross,					
Per dozen,					

SOUP PLATES.

	Per gross.	Per dozen.
9 inch,		
10 "		

SCOLLOPED PIE PLATES.

Inches,		7	8	9	9
Deep,	in.	1¼	1 5/16	1⅜	2
Per gross,					
Per dozen,					

ALPHABET or CHILDREN'S PLATES.

No.	1	2	3	4
Inches,	4½	5	5½	6
Per gross,				
Per dozen,				

WASHINGTON PIE or JELLY CAKE PANS.

Inches,		8	9	10
Deep,	in.	½	½	½
Per gross,				
Per dozen,				

CAKE PANS.

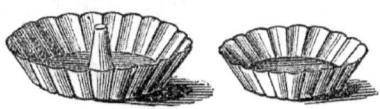 

Per gross. Per dozen.

Scolloped, No. 1, large, with tube, 9½ inches, ...
" " 2, small, " 8 " . . . .
" " 1, large, without tube, 9½ " . . . .
" " 2, small, " 8 " . . . .
" " 3, " " 6½ " . . . .
Octagon, " 1, large, with tube, 9½ " . . . .
" " 2, small, " 8 " . . . .
" " 1, large, without tube, 9½ " . . . .
" " 2, small, " 8 " . . . .
Plain Round, No. 1, large, with tube, 9¾ " . . . .
" " 2, small, " 8¼ " . . . .
Extra large Scolloped, with tube, ...

WASH BOWLS.

STAMPED.

FEET LOOSE.	FEET FASTENED ON.
Per gross. Per doz.	Per gross. Per doz.
No. 1, small, 9½ in. .	No. 1, small, 9½ in. .
2, med. 11¼ " .	2, med. 11¼ " .
3, large, 13 " .	3, large, 13 " .

Flat Bottom, French Pattern.

Per gross. Per doz.

No. 1, small, 9½ inches, ...
2, med. 11½ " . . . .

For heavy triple Tinned Iron Basins, see French Ware.

PATTIES.
Washington Scollops.

	Per gross.	Per doz.
Deep, No. 1, 2¾ in.		
" " 2, 3⅛ "		
" " 3, 3½ "		

Scollop Patties.

	Per gross.	Per doz.
No. 1, 3 inches,		
2, 3½ "		
3, 4 "		
4, 4½ "		
5, 5 "		
6, 5½ "		

Plain Patties.

	Per gross.	Per doz.
No. 1, 3 inches,		
2, 3½ "		
3, 4 "		
4, 4½ "		
5, 5 "		
6, 5½ "		
7, 6 "		

Heart Scollops.

	Per gross.	Per doz.
No. 1, 2⅞ inches,		
2, 3½ "		

Star Scollops.

	Per gross.	Per doz.
No. 1, 3¼ inches,		
2, 3½ "		

Shell Scollops.

	Per gross.	Per doz.
No. 1,		
2,		

Oblong Sq. Scollops.

	Per gross.	Per doz.
No. 1, 3 x4 in.		
2, 2¾x3¾ "		

ROUND STAMPED MILK PANS.

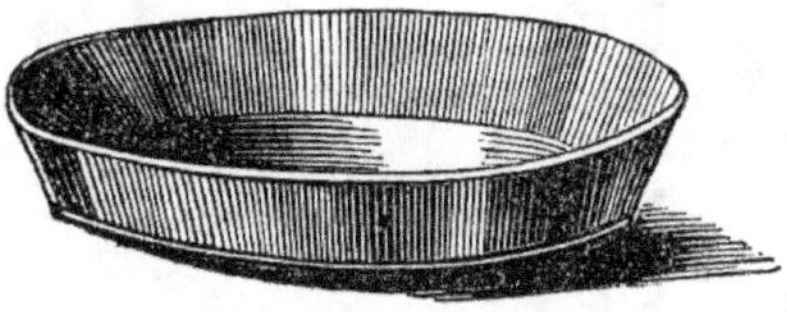

Pints, .		½	*1*	*2*	*3*	*Quarts,* .	*2*	*3*	*4*	*6*	*10*
Across Top, .	in.	4¾	6	7	8¼		9	9¾	11¼	13	15¾
Across bottom,	in.	3	3¾	4¾	5½		6	6¾	7¾	9½	11¾
Deep, . . .	in.	1⅜	1⅝	1¾	2		2⅛	2⅜	2⅝	2⅞	3⅛
Per gross, .											
Per dozen, .											

OVAL PANS.

	Per gross.	Per dozen.
12 inches, ...		
14 "		

STAMPED DIPPERS.

WITH HANDLE.

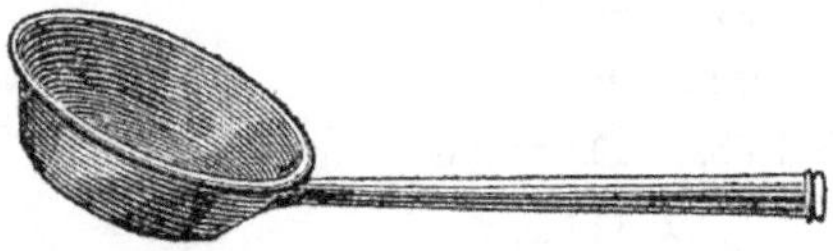

Pints, ...	½	1	2
Per gross, ...			
Per dozen, ...			

DIPPER BOWLS.

	Per gross.	Per dozen.
½ Pint, ...		
1 "		
1 Quart, ...		

E. L. PARKER & CO., BALTIMORE.

Cake Cutters.

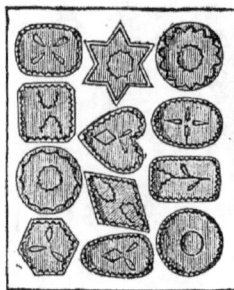

Oak Leaf Cake Cutters.

Per gross. Per doz

No. 1, ...

2, ...

3, ...

The filling of these corresponds with the fancy, but are not assorted.

Per gross. Per doz.

No. 1, Assorted, . .

2, " . .

3, " . .

The cut represents No. 2. No. 1, has more, and No. 3, less fancy filling. Each dozen has the variety represented.

Biscuit Cutters.

Per gross. Per doz

No. 1, ...

2, ...

Square Bread and Drip Pans.

Per gross. Per dozen.

No. 1, 1 inch shallow, 10x14 inches, ...

2, 1½ " " 10x14 " . . . . .

Bread, No. 1, 2 inches deep, 10x14 inches, ...

" " 2, 2½ " " 10x14 " . . . . .

" " 1, 2 " " 14x20 " . . . . .

Gravy Strainers.

Per gross. Per dozen.

No. 1, 4 inches on top, ...

2, 4⅝ " " . . . .

3, 5 " . . . .

MONROE'S
Patent Egg Beater.

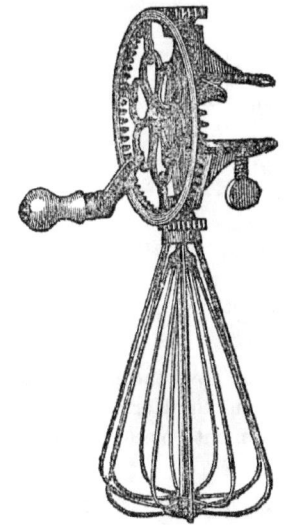

Per dozen.

Family Size, ...
Mammoth, for Hotels and Bakers, ...

EARLE'S
Patent Egg Beater.

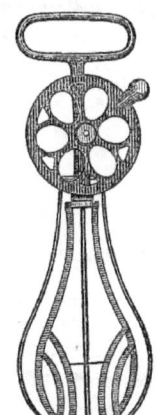

Per dozen.

No. 1, ...

This, while it is the simplest, is the most effective Egg Beater made. Held in the hand with an immovable rest, it stands firmly wherever placed, and will beat eggs with greater rapidity than any other; while the price places it within the reach of all. It is cleaned by a moment's rapid turning in hot water.

LANTERNS.

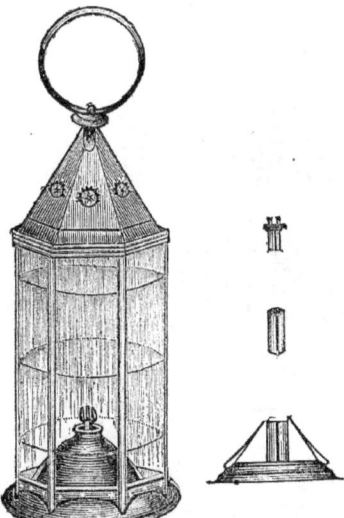

Per dozen.

No. 1, Parker's Sq., Oil and Candles, .
    1,   "   "   Kerosene and Candles, ...
No. 1, Globe, Kerosene, ...
    2,   "   "   . . . . . .
    3,   "   "   . . . . . .
    1, Egg,   "   . . . . . .
    2,   "   "   . . . . . .
    3,   "   "   . . . . . .
    1,   "   for Candle, ...
    1, Hexagon, Kerosene and Candle,
    1,   "   Common Oil and Candle, ...
    1, Hexagon, Candle only, ...

Egg Whips.

	Per dozen.
No. 1, Wood Handle,	. . .
2, " "	. . .
1, Tin "	. . .

Soap Dishes.

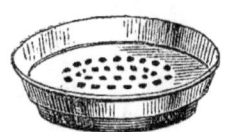

	Per dozen.
No. 1, Wood, 5½ in.	. . .
1, Tinned Iron, 5¼ in.	. .

Patent Fluted Funnels.

	Per dozen.
No. 1,	. . . .
2,	. . . .
3,	. . . .
4,	. . . .

Horns.

	Per dozen.
Patent, No. 1,	. . . . .
Common, No. 1,	. . . .
" " 2,	. . . .
" " 3,	. . . .
Fisher, C.	. . . . . .
" L.	. . . . . .
Extra mouth pieces per package C,	. . . .
Extra mouth pieces per package L,	. . . .

C and L have the mouth pieces detached from the Horns; the C has 17, and L 18 mouth pieces to the dozen.

Round Oyster Blazers.

	Per dozen.
9 inch Pan,	. . . . . .

JELLY MOULDS.

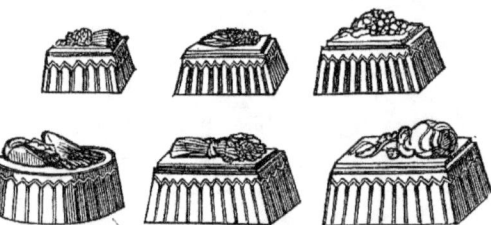

Pints.	½	1	1½	2
Per gross, ...				
Per dozen, ...				

Patent Threaded Basting Spoons.

TINNED.

	SOLID.						RIVETED.					
Inches,	10	12	14	16	18	20	10	12	14	16	18	20
Per dozen,												

Forged Basting Spoons.

TINNED.

Inches, ...	10	12	14	16	18	20
Per dozen, ...						

Tinned Iron Basting Spoons.

FLAT AND ROUND HANDLED.

Inches, ...	10	12	14	16	18	20	22	24
Per dozen, ...								

TEA SPOONS.—Threaded.

TINNED.

No.	305	310	117	31	30	32
Inches,	5¾	5¾	5¾	5¾	6	6
Per gross,						

TABLE SPOONS.

Per gross. Per dozen.

Threaded Riveted, No. 200, 7½ inches, ...
"   "   " 210, 7¾   "   . . . . .
"   Solid,   "   20, 7½   "   . . . . .
"   "   "   21, 7¾   "   . . . . .
"   "   "   40, 7½   "   . . . . .
"   "   "   41, 7¾   "   . . . . .
"   Riveted, N. P., No. 222, ...
"   Solid,   "   " 216, ...
"   Patent, No. 50, ...

Patent Threaded Table Forks.

TINNED.

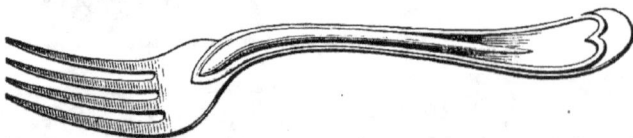

Per gross. Per dozen.

No. 24, 7½ inches, ...

TEA SPOONS.

	Per gross.	Per dozen.
Flat Handle, No. 3,		
Round " " 85,		
Patent Round Handle, Riveted, No. 9½		
Patent, No. 50,		

BRITANNIA SPOONS.

WIRE STRENGTHENED.

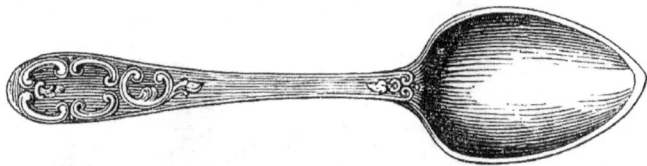

TEA.

	Per gross.	Per dozen.
Plain, No. 6900,		
Fiddle, " 35,		
Threaded, No. 80,		
Brunswick,		

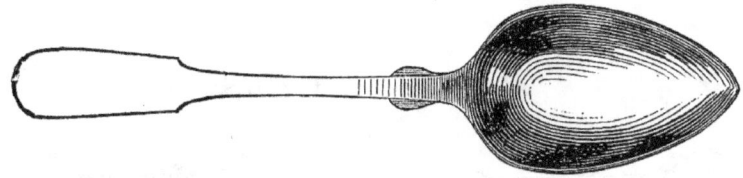

TABLE.

	Per gross.	Per dozen.
Plain, No. 1390,		
Fiddle, " 70,		
Threaded, No. 90,		
Brunswick,		

ALBATA METAL.

BRUNSWICK PATTERN.

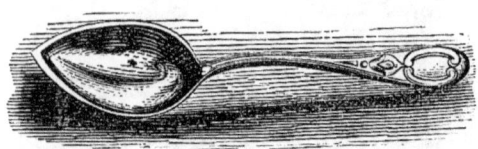

TEA.

                                          Per gross. Per dozen.

Threaded Tip'd, ...
Olive, ...
Brunswick, ...

ALBATA METAL.

THREADED PATTERN.

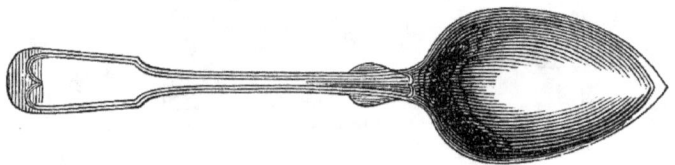

TABLE.

                                          Per gross. Per dozen.

Threaded Tip'd, ...
Olive, ...
Brunswick, ...

PASTE JAGGERS.

                                        Per gross. Per dozen.

No. 10, Metallic, ...
    1. Wood Handle, ...
    2,   "   Wheel, ...

CAKE TURNERS.

THREADED HANDLES.

			WOOD HANDLE.	
No.	15	16	17	18
Inches,	4	4½	4	4½
Per gross,				
Per dozen,				

CAKE TURNERS.—Wood Handles.

TINNED.

No. 5, ... Per gross. Per dozen.   No. 10, Wood Handle,   Per gross. Per dozen.

CAKE TURNERS.—Wood Handles.

STEEL AND IRON.

	STEEL.		IRON.
No.	1	2	3
Per gross,			
Per dozen,			

E. L. PARKER & CO., BALTIMORE. 57

SHERWOOD'S PATENT CORRUGATED
WIRE GAUZE STRAINERS,

A variety of convenient and ornamental articles, neatly made from a beautiful and superior quality of Fine Corrugated Wire Gauze, both of TIN and heavy SILVER PLATE.

TEA OR COFFEE STRAINERS.

Per dozen.
Tinned, No. 1, 1¾ inch, ...
Silver Plated, No. 1, 1¾ inch, ... ; . . .

These Strainers separate the dregs from Tea or Coffee thoroughly, and are great savers of Tea, Coffee and Sugar, as by their use this beverage is made so clear that no part need be wasted. Applied or detached in a moment.

URN OR FAUCET STRAINERS.

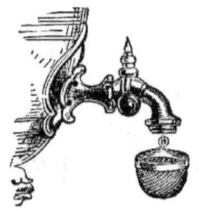 

	TINNED.		SILVER PLATED.	
No.	1	2	1	2
Inches, ...	1¾	2⅛	1¾	2⅛
Per dozen, . . .				

These are different (notice spring and bail) from those to be applied to Tea or Coffee Pots, yet are to be applied similar to the above, to Tea or Coffee Urns, Water Faucets, &c.

HANDLE STRAINERS.

THREE SIZES.

	TINNED.			SILVER PLATED.		
No.	1	2	3	1	2	3
Inches,	2½	3⅛	3⅞	2½	3⅛	3⅞
Per dozen,						

These are for Straining Nursery and Fancy Drinks, Starch, Yeast, Blanc-Manges, Custards, Gravies, Syrups, Jellies, and for Sifting Sugar upon Fruit, Cake, Pies, &c. Also, for Sifting Salt into Butter.

SHERWOOD'S WIRE DISH STANDS.

BEAUTIFULLY PLATED WITH PURE TIN.

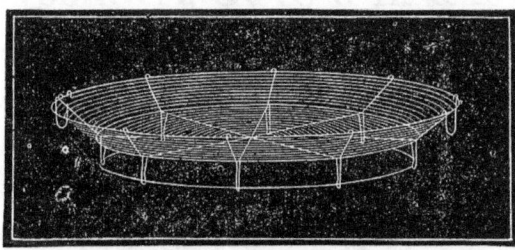

Are a very neat and durable kind of Table Mats, having the appearance of little raised stands of silver filagree work, upon which may be received from the fire hot dishes of food, serving the double purpose of

Dish Holders and Table Mats.

Dishes, however hot, may be received upon them, carried to, and placed upon the table—the Stands fully protecting the hands from heat in carrying, and the table and cloth from heat and soiling.

They are also very convenient for holding dishes when desired to place the same in water or elsewhere to cool, as they allow the cold air or water to circulate freely beneath them.

The smallest size makes a nice stand for tea and coffee pots, and all sizes are also used by many as Dish Covers. As Fruit Dishes they have great beauty and excellence.

Put up in packages of one dozen.

FOUR SIZES.   Round.   Oval.

No. 1, 7½ inches diameter at the top, per dozen, ...
    2, 8½   "   "   "   "   . . . .
    3, 9½   "   "   "   "   . . . .
    4, 10½   "   "   "   "   . . . .

E. L. PARKER & CO., BALTIMORE.

SHERWOOD'S PATENT WIRE EGG STANDS.

BEAUTIFULLY PLATED WITH PURE TIN.

 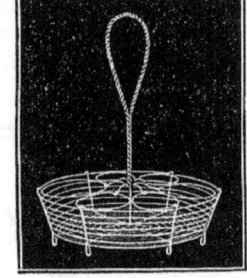

SIZE.   Per gross. Per dozen.

No. 4, Four Eggs, ...
    6, Six Eggs, ...
    8, Eight Eggs, ...
   12, Twelve Eggs, ...

(No. 12 has 2 tiers of holes—8 below and 4 above.)

These stands are used in boiling Eggs, and also as Egg Holders upon the table. Put up in Paper Boxes of *half a dozen* of one size.

ROUND AND OVAL WIRE COVERS.

ROUND.

Inches,	6	7	8	9	10	11	12	14	16	18
Per dozen,										

OVAL.

Inches,	6	7	8	9	10	11	12	14	16	18
Per dozen,										

PATENT UNION BOX MILL.

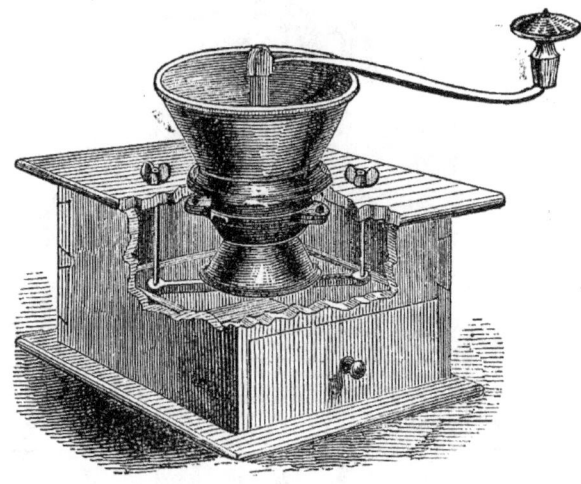

THREE STYLES, ALL OF ONE SIZE.

Per dozen.

Oak, No 25, with Iron Hopper, ...
Walnut, No. 40, with Iron Hopper, ...
Oak, No. 35, with Britannia Hopper, ...
Walnut, No. 45, with Britannia Hopper, ...

Parker's Patent Eagle Box Mills.

IRON HOPPERS.

No.	101	102	103	104
Per dozen,				

BRITANNIA HOPPERS.

No.	105	106	107	108
Per dozen,				

BOX COFFEE OR SPICE MILL.

IN HALF DOZEN BOXES.

No.	IRON HOPPER.				BRITANNIA HOPPER.		
	1	2	3	4	1	2	3
Per dozen,							

SIDE COFFEE MILLS.

No.	0	1	2	3	50	60	70	80
Per dozen,								

WILSON'S, ... per dozen.

SHOVELS—Wood Handles.

HEAVY SHEET IRON.

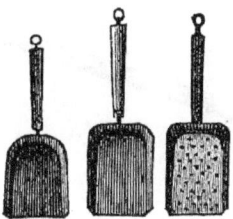

CAST IRON.

BLADE.   Per gross. Per dozen.

No. 18, 7¼ x 5¼ inches, Wood Handle, ...
    23, 7¼ x 5¼   "   "   " . . . . .
     1, Common, ...
     1, Wood Handle, ...
     2,   "   "   " . . . . .
     1, Cinder, Wood Handle, ...
     1, Cast Iron, ...

IRON HANDLE COAL SHOVELS.

JAPANNED.

Per gross. Per dozen.

No. 1, Common, ...
     2,   " . . . .
Light, No. 0, L. & G., 6½ inches, ...
   "   "   00,   "   7¾   " . . . . .
   "   "   01,   "   7¾   " . . . . .
No. 1, L. & G., 7¾ inches, ...
     2,   "   8¾   " . . . . .
     6, Cinder, 7¾ inches, ...

Long Iron Handled Coal Shovels.

JAPANNED.

L. & G.

			CINDER.	
No.	4	5	8	9
Inches,	7¾	8¾	7¾	8¾
Per dozen,				

Wood Handled Coal Shovels.

JAPANNED.

L. & G.

	SOCKET SHANK.		FERRULED.		
No.	10	20	90	100	200
Inches,	7¾	8¾	7¾	7¾	8¾
Per dozen,					

Patent Wood Handle Cover Lifters.

	Per dozen.		Per dozen.
No. 1, ...		No. 2, Patent,	. . .

These are manufactured of tough iron, and the wooden handle is securely fastened. They are cheap and durable.

STOVE POKERS.

	COMMON.			WOOD HANDLE.
No.	1	2	3	1
Inches, ...	15	17	19	19
Per dozen, . . .				

COAL HODS.

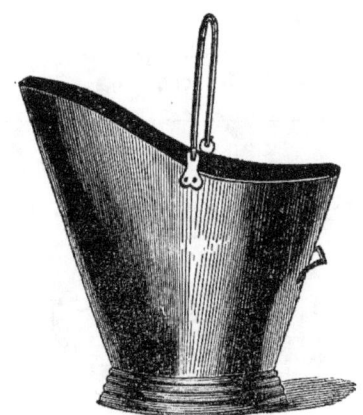

	BLACK.					GALVANIZED.				
Inches, . . .	14	15	16	17	18	14	15	16	17	18
Per dozen, . . .										

FIRE CARRIERS.

JAPANNED.

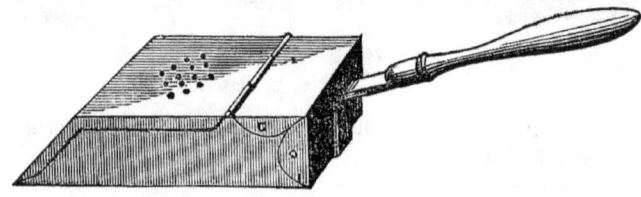

No.	1	18
Per dozen,		

SAD IRONS.

FINE FINISH.

Per pound.

No. 1, from 4 to 10 pounds, sharp points, ...
    1, " 4 to 10 " round " . . . . .
Saleable Sizes, assorted, in cases of about 200 pounds, ...
    " " " barrels " 700 " . . . .

SAD IRON STANDS.

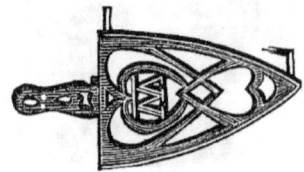

No.	1	2
Per gross,		
Per dozen,		

COFFEE POT STANDS.

JAPANNED.		PLAIN.	
No.	1	No.	2
Per dozen, ...		Per dozen, . . .	

FRY PANS.

COMMON.

No.	0	1	2	3	4	5	6	7	8
Inches on top, .	8	8¾	9¼	10	10½	11	12	13	14
Per dozen, . .	2 81	3 00	3 38	3 75	4 12	4 50	5 00	5 62	6 75

POLISHED.

No.	0	1	2	3	4	5	6	7	8
Inches on top, .	8	8½	9	9½	10	11	12	13	14
Per dozen, . .									

E. L. PARKER & CO., BALTIMORE.

ENGLISH HAMMERED
WROUGHT IRON BAKE PANS.

ROUND.

Inches on top, . .	9	9½	10	10½	11	11½	12	12½	13
Per pound, . . .									

OVAL.

Inches long on top, .	9	9½	10	10½	11	11½
Per pound, ...						
Inches long on top, .	12	12½	13	14	14½	15
Per pound, ...						

OBLONG SQUARE.

Inches long on top, .	13¾	15½	16½	18	18½	19
Inches wide on top,	8½	10	10¾	11¾	12¼	13
Per pound, . . .						

OCTAGON COFFEE POTS.—Black Handle.

BURNISHED TOP.

Pints,	2	3	4	5	6	8
Per dozen,						

PLAIN COFFEE POTS.

Quarts,	1	1½	2	3	4	5	6
Per dozen,							

COFFEE BOILERS.

						BAILED.
Quarts, 1½	2	3	4	5	6	8
Per dozen,						

OCTAGON COFFEE BIGGINS.—Black Handle.

BURNISHED COVER.

Pints,	2	3	4	6
Each,				
Per dozen,				

ROUND TEA POTS.—Black Handle.

BURNISHED TOP.

Pints,	2	3	4	5	6
Per dozen,					

ROUND TEA POTS.—Tin Handle.

Pints,	2	3	4	5	6
Per dozen,					

OCTAGON TEA POTS.—*Black Handle.*

BURNISHED TOP.

Pints,	2	3	4	5	6	8
Per dozen,						

PLANISHED
TEA AND COFFEE POTS.

No.	700	710	720	730	740	
Per dozen,						

OVAL TEA POTS.—Black Handle.

Pints, . . .	2	3	4	5	6
Per dozen, . . .					

PLANISHED

TEA AND COFFEE POTS.

WITH BRITANNIA TOP AND HANDLE.

No.	30	40	50	60	70	
Per dozen, . .						

PLANISHED
ROUND COFFEE POTS.

Pints, . . .	2	3	4	5	6	8
Per dozen, . .						

BRITANNIA POTS.

FINE ROLLED METAL POTS, WITH TINNED FIRE-PROOF BOTTOMS.

No.	1400	1410	1420	1430	1440
Pints, ...	3½	4	7½	9	10
Per dozen, . . .					

JAPANNED WARE,

A Full and Varied Assortment.

WATER COOLERS,

In all Varieties.

TOILET SETS,

Tastefully Ornamented and Handsomely Finished.

JAPANNED WARE.

WATER COOLERS.

Gallons, each, . .	1½	2	3	4	5	6	8	10
Per dozen, ...								

Highly ornamented, and made in the best manner, with Galvanized Iron Ice Chamber, and first class Faucet, tastefully ornamented, in various styles and colors.

"CORRUGATED."

WITH PLATED FAUCETS.

Gallons, each,	1½	2	3	4	6	8	10
Per dozen, . .							

This cut represents the Cooler as if cut in half, and shows the Patent Corrugated Bottom in the cylinder of Cooler.

WATER PAILS.

ASSORTED COLORS.

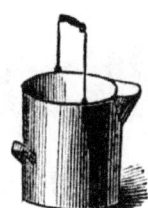

No.	1	2	3	4	COVERED.			
					1	2	3	4
Quarts, ...	8	10	12	14	8	10	12	14
Per dozen, ...								

SLOP OR CHAMBER PAILS.

VARIOUS COLORS, PLAIN GREEN, OAK, PANELLED, &C., &C.

No.		100	250	350	1	2	3	4	5
Diam. of Breast, .	in.	12¼	11¼	10					
Per dozen, . . .									

TOILET WARE.

THREE PIECES.

No. 1, SETS.

Per set.

No. 10, Plain Green,
French Gray,
Oak,
Oak and Mahogany,
Black Walnut,
Panelled, (oval carrier)

And various other styles.

No. 2, SETS.

No. 1, Extra Finish, (oval carrier)
8, Peacock,
15, Green, Filleted and Flowered,
20, Imitation of Oak and Rosewood,
30, Imitation of Grapes,
35, White, Filleted Rose,
40, Drab, Ornamented,
41, Dark Pink, Ornamented, (circlet)
50, Drab, Ornamented,
60, Blue, Filleted Rose,
72, Maroon, Filleted Rose,
80, Imitation of Rosewood,
103, Black, Filleted and Flowered,
115, Green, Flowers and Gilt, (circlet)
140, Drab, " " "
203, Black, " " "
215, Green, " " "

EXTRA FINE.

No. 100, Crimson, Drapery and Flowered, fancy,
101, Blue, " " "
102, Green, " " "

And various other styles and colors.

TOILET WARE.

WITH LIPPED PAIL.

Per set.

No. 1, Panelled,
    1, Extra Finish,
  095, Drab, Ornamented,
  096, White, "
  097, Green, "
   98, Imitation Oak,

TOILET BOWLS AND PITCHERS.

TO MATCH TOILET SETS.

Per set.	Per set.
No. 1, Large,	No. 1, Small,
15, A, Large,	10, B, Small,
40, A, "	15, B, "
50, A, "	40, B, "
100, A, "	50, B, "
101, A, "	
102, A, "	

OVAL FOOT TUBS.

	PLAIN GREEN.			PANELLED DRAB.		
No.	1	2	3	1	2	3
Per dozen, ...						

HIP OR SIZE BATHS.

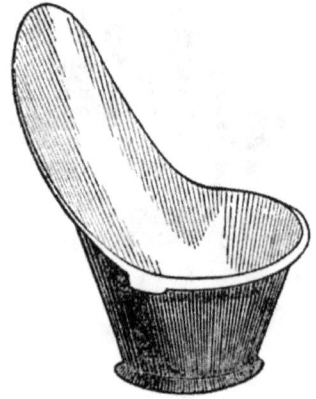

Each.

Tin, Japanned, ...
Zinc, " . . . .

CHILDREN'S BATHS.

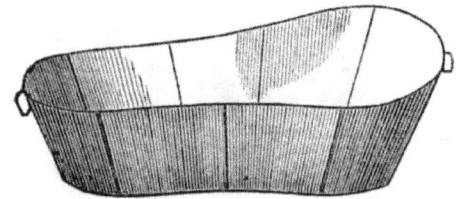

No.	1	2	3	4	5	6
Inches on Top, length,	28	30	32	38	40	42
Each,						

SPONGING BATHS.

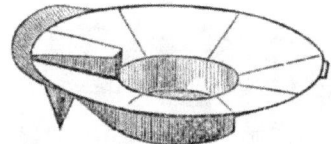

Each, ...

SUGAR BOXES.

No.	1	2	3	4	5	6
Nest of	3	4	5	6	7	8
Per nest,						

SUGAR BOWLS, ... per dozen,

CAKE BOXES.

Per nest.

Round, 3 in Nest,
Square, 3 "

CASH BOXES.

WITH LOCK AND KEY.

	WITH TRAY.					WITHOUT TRAY.		
No.	1	2	3	4	5	1	2	3
Inches,	12x8	10½x7	9x6			12x8	10¼x7	9x6
Per gross,								
Per dozen,								

WITHOUT TRAY.

No.	1	2	3	4	5	6
Inches,	13½	11½	10½	9½	8½	7½
Per gross,						
Per dozen,						

DEED BOXES.

WITH HASP.

No.	1	2	3
Inches,	12x8	10½x7	9x6
Per gross,			
Per dozen,			

TRUNKS.

BRASS HANDLE.

Nest of	3	4	5	6	7
Per nest,					

SPICE BOXES.

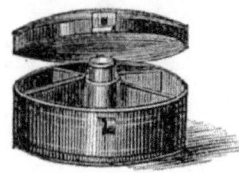

Per gross. Per dozen.

Square, 9½ inches, Stamped Top, Sq. Boxes inside, . . .
" 10½ " " " " " . . .
" 9½ " " " " Round, Boxes inside, . . .
" 9½ " Flat Top, Sq. Boxes inside, . . .
Desk Top, 9½ inches, ...
Round, No. 1, 8¼ inches, ...
" " 2, 6½ " . . . .

TEA AND COFFEE CANS.

Pounds,	$\frac{1}{4}$	$\frac{1}{2}$	1	2	3	4	6	8
Per gross,								
Per dozen,								

SQUARE.

Pounds,	2	4	6	8	10	12	14	16
Per gross,								
Per dozen,								

TEA AND COFFEE CANS.

HINGED TOP.

Pounds,	1	$1\frac{1}{2}$	2	3
Per gross,				
Per dozen,				

GROCERY CANISTERS.

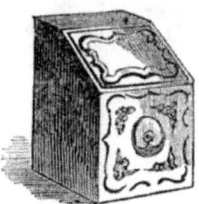

SLANTING TOP.

	SMALL.	MEDIUM.	LARGE.
Pounds, ...	*8*	*12*	*16*
Per gross, ...			
Per dozen, ...			

FORK AND SPOON BOXES.

FLANNEL LINED.

Per gross. Per dozen.

No. 1, 9¾ inches Square, ...

KNIFE AND FORK BOXES.

FLANNEL LINED.

Per gross. Per dozen.

12½ inches Long, ...

KNIFE TRAY.

No.	0	1	2	3
Per gross,				
Per dozen,				

TUMBLER DRAINER.

No.	1	2	3	5	6
Inches,	5x8	$7\frac{1}{2}$x$11\frac{1}{2}$	9x13	$10\frac{1}{2}$x15	$12\frac{1}{2}$x20
Per gross,					
Per dozen,					

NURSERY LAMPS.

Per dozen.

Common,	
Fancy,	
Plain Perf., with Tea Kettle,	
Colored, with Tea Kettle,	

CANDLESTICKS.

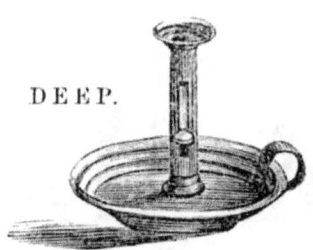
DEEP.

	JAPANNED.			FANCY.
No.	1	2	3	1
Per gross,				
Per dozen,				

	PLAIN SHALLOW.		PLAIN DEEP	
No.	1	2	1	2
Per gross,				
Per dozen,				

BRASS CHAMBER.

No.	1	2	3
Inches,	5	5½	6
Per dozen pair,			

PLANISHED.

No.	1	2	3
Per gross,			
Per dozen,			

LAMPS AND LANTERNS.

Per gross. Per doz.

Jacket Lamp, ...
Extra Jacket Lamp, ...
Stand Lamp, ...
Small Folding Pocket Lantern, ...
Large " " " . . . .

	POLICE.		OPEN POCKET.			DARK POCKET.		
No.	1	2	1	2	3	1	2	3
Per gross,								
Per dozen,								

COVERED BUCKETS.

PLAIN. TIN.

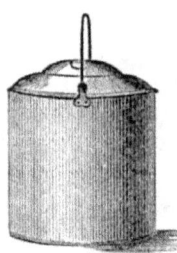

Quarts,	½	1	2	3	4	6	8	10	12
Per dozen,									

DUST PANS.

Per gross. Per dozen.

No. 1, Small, Japanned, ...
    2, Large,   "   . . . .
    2, "   Plain, ...
    2, "   Japanned, Corrugated, ...
    2, "   "   Fancy, ...
    2, "   "   Half Covered, ...

SPITTOONS.

PLAIN AND HINGE TOP.

No.		1	2	3
Wide and Deep,	in.	8x3	8x2½	8x2
Per gross,				
Per dozen,				

Japanned Wash Bowls.

PAINTED INSIDE.

	Per gross.	Per dozen.
Small, 9½ inches,		
Medium, 11¼ inches,		
Large, 12¾ inches,		

MOLASSES CUPS.

Pints,	½	1	Quarts,	1	2
Per gross,			Per gross,		
Per dozen,			Per dozen,		

Pepper Boxes.   ### *Flour or Dredge Boxes.*

	Per gross.	Per dozen.		Per gross.	Per doz.
Small,			Plain, No. 1,		
Large,			Japanned, No. 1,		
			Japanned, No. 2,		

MATCH SAFES.

 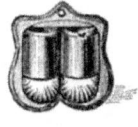 

	Per gross.	Per doz.		Per gross.	Per doz.
No. 1, Square,			Kline's Self-Closing,		
2, "			Round, No. 1,		
Twin, No. 1,			" " 2,		
" " 2.			Square Iron, No. 1,		
Stella,			" " " 2,		

Patent Graters.

	Per gross.	Per doz.
No. 1,		

Radial Graters.

	Per gross.	Per doz.
No. 1,		

Box Graters.

	Per gross.	Per doz.
No. 1,		

Bottom Graters.

	Per gross.	Per doz.
No. 1,		

Japanned Tumblers.

	Per gross.	Per doz.
½ Pint,		
1 "		
1 Quart,		

Sugar Bowls.

	Per gross.	Per doz.
No. 1,		
2,		

JAPANNED TIN TOYS.

Straight Toy Cups.

	Per gross.	Per doz.
No. 1,		
2,		
3,		
4,		
5,		

Flaring Toy Cups.

	Per gross.	Per doz.
No. 1, Large,		
2, Medium,		
3, Small,		

House Banks.

Per gross. Per doz.
No. 1, Large, . . .
    2, Small, . . .
Sq. No. 1, Large, .
"   "   2, Small, .

Gothic Banks.

Per gross. Per doz.
No. 1, Large, . . .
    2, Small, . . .

Toy Covered Pails.

  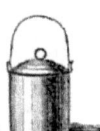

Per gross. Per doz.
No. 1, Large, . . .
    2, Medium, . .
    3, Small, . . .

Scholars' Companions.

Per gross. Per doz.
No. 1, ...
    2, ...

Assorted Animals.

Per gro. Per doz.
Lion, Tiger, Leopard, Cow, }
  Horse and Elephant,   }
In one Package, ...

Toy Buckets.

VARIOUS COLORS.

Per gross. Per doz.
No. 1, Largest, . .
    2, ...
    3, ...
    4, ...
    5, ...
    6, ...

Rattles and Whistles.

Per gross. Per doz.
No. 1, ...

Coffee and Tea Pots.

Per gross. Per doz.
Coffee, ...
Tea, ...

Oval Butter Kettles.

Per gross. Per doz.
No. 152, ...
    153, ...
    153½, ...

Bow Carts.

Per gross. Per doz.
No. 51, ...
    101, ...
    102, ...

FRENCH
STAMPED TINNED IRON WARE,
&c., &c.

SAUCEPANS, BASINS, BUCKETS,

DISH PANS,

&c., &c.

SHALLOW STEW PANS.
TINNED.

No.	1	2	3	4	5	6	8	10
Quarts,	$\frac{1}{2}$	1	$1\frac{1}{2}$	2	3	4	6	10
Inches,	$5\frac{3}{4}$x$1\frac{1}{2}$	$6\frac{3}{4}$x2	$7\frac{1}{2}$x$2\frac{1}{4}$	$8\frac{1}{4}$x$2\frac{1}{4}$	9x$2\frac{1}{2}$	$10\frac{1}{4}$x$2\frac{5}{8}$	$12\frac{1}{4}$x$2\frac{3}{4}$	15x3
Per dozen,								

DEEP STEW PANS.
TINNED.

No.	16	18	20	22	24	26	28	30	32	36
Quarts,	2	$2\frac{1}{2}$	3	4	5	6	$7\frac{1}{2}$	$9\frac{1}{2}$	$11\frac{1}{2}$	$13\frac{1}{2}$
Inches,	$6\frac{1}{2}$x3	$7\frac{1}{2}$x3	8x$3\frac{1}{2}$	$8\frac{3}{4}$x$3\frac{1}{2}$	$9\frac{3}{4}$x4	$10\frac{1}{4}$x$4\frac{3}{4}$	$10\frac{3}{4}$x$4\frac{3}{4}$	$11\frac{1}{2}$x$5\frac{1}{4}$	$12\frac{1}{2}$x$5\frac{1}{2}$	$13\frac{1}{2}$x6
Per dozen,										

LIGHT LIPPED SAUCEPANS.

TINNED.

No.	010	012	014	016	018	020	022	024	026	028
Quarts,	¾	1	1½	2	2½	3	4	5	6	7½
Inches,	5x2½	6 3¼	6½x3½	7¼x3¾	7¾x4	8¼x4¼	9x4¾	9¾x5¼	10½x5½	11½x6
Per dozen,										

STRONG SAUCEPANS.

TINNED.

No.	16	18	20	22	24	26	28	30	32	36
Quarts,	2	2½	3½	4½	5½	6½	8	10	12	14
Inches,	6¾ 4	7¾ 4	8½x4¼	9¼x4½	10¼x4¾	10¾x5¼	11¼x5¼	12x6	13x6	14x6½
Per dozen,										

CHAMBER PAILS.

TINNED.

No.	1	2	3
Quarts,		3	
Inches,		12x10	
Per dozen,			

MILK PAILS.

TINNED.

No.	4	5	6
Quarts,		3	
Inches,		12½x8	
Per dozen,			

WATER PAILS.
TINNED.

No.	7	8	9	10	11	12
Gallons,		2	3		6	8
Inches,		10½x7	12½x8		16x9	17¾x10½
Per dozen,						

FRUIT OR WASH KETTLES.
TINNED.

No.	13	14	15	16	17
Gallons,	2	3		6	8
Inches,	10½x7	12½x8		16x9	17¾x10½
Per dozen,					

SHALLOW PRESERVING KETTLES.

TINNED.

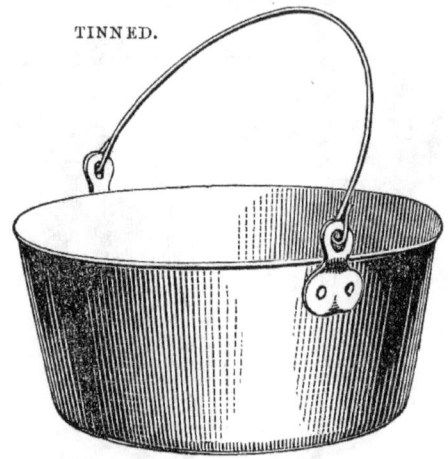

No.	016	018	020	022	024	026	028	030	032	036
Quarts,	2	2½	3	4	5	6	7½	9½	11½	13½
Inches,	6½x3	7½x3	8x3½	8¾x3½	9¾x4	10¼x4¾	10¾x4¾	11½x5¼	12½x5½	13½x6
Per dozen,										

DEEP PRESERVING KETTLES.

TINNED.

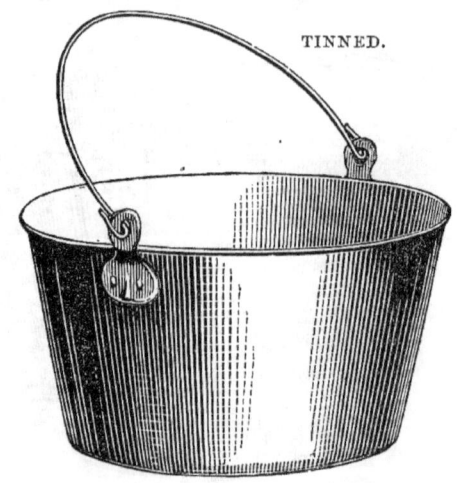

No.	16	18	20	22	24	26	28	30	32	36
Quarts,	2	2½	3½	4½	5½	6½	8	10	12	14
Inches,	7x3¾	7¾x4	8½x4¼	9¼x4½	10x4¾	10¾x5	11½x5¼	12½x5½	13x5¾	14¼x6
Per dozen,										

MEDIUM DISH PANS.

TINNED.

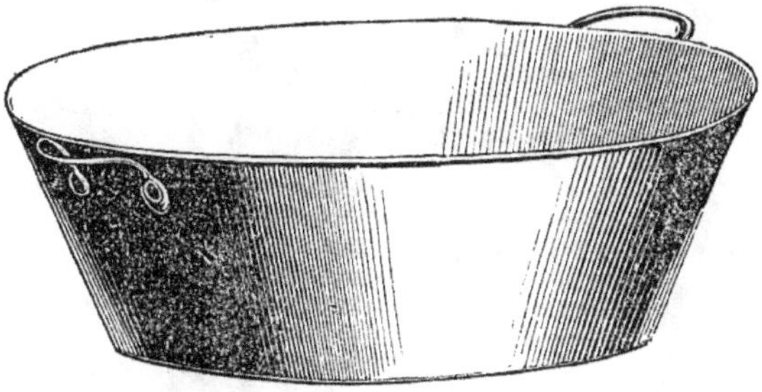

No.	***0½***	***1½***	***2½***	***3½***	***4½***
Quarts, ...	8	10	14	20	30
Inches, ...	13x4½	15x4½	16½x5	20x6	22x6
Per dozen, . . .					

DEEP DISH PANS.

TINNED.

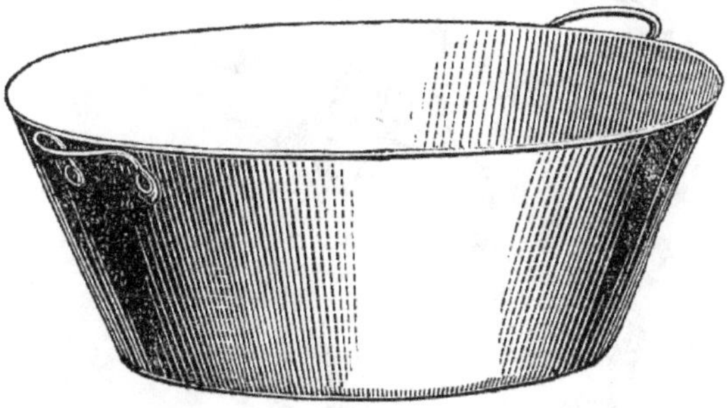

No.	***0***	***1***	***2***	***3***	***4***
Quarts, ...	8	10	14	20	30
Inches, ...	12¾x5½	14½x5½	15¼x6¼	18¾x6¾	21x7
Per dozen, . . .					

TEA KETTLES.

No.	1	2	3	4
Quarts,	2	4	5	6
Per dozen,				

TEA KETTLES.

No.				
Quarts,				
Per dozen,				

STRONG BAKE PANS.

POLISHED.

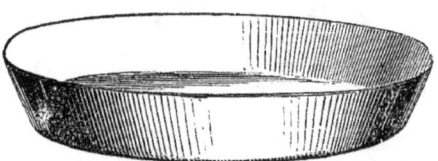

No.	0	1	2	3	4	5	6	7	8
Inches,	8	8½	9	9½	10	11	12	13	14
Per dozen,									

DEEP FRY PANS.

TINNED.

No.	0	1	2	3	4	5	6	7	8
Inches,	8	8½	9	9½	10	11	12	13	14
Per dozen,									

DEEP FRY PANS.

POLISHED.

No.	0	1	2	3	4	5	6	7	8
Inches,	8	8½	9	9½	10	11	12	13	14
Per dozen,									

GRIDIRONS.

TINNED.

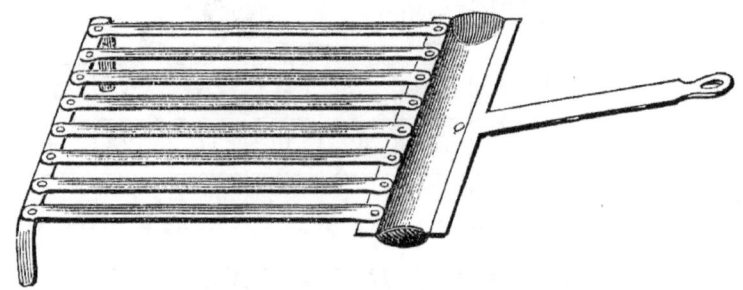

No.	6	7	8	9	10	11	12
Inches,	10	10½	11½	12½	13½	14½	15
Per dozen,							

CULLENDERS.

TINNED.

FEET LOOSE.

	STRONG.			LIGHT.	STRONG.
No.	1	2	3	05	5
Inches,	9½	10¾	12¾	10¾	10¾
Per dozen,					

FRENCH WASH BASINS.

TINNED.

	MEDIUM.			LIGHT.		
No......	024	026	028	12	13	14
Inches, ...	9¾	10½	11	9¾	10½	11
Per dozen, ...						

WASH BASINS.

TINNED.

FEET LOOSE.

	STRONG.			LIGHT.		
No.....	1	2	3	01	02	03
Inches, ...	9½	10¾	12¾	9½	10¾	12¾
Per dozen, ..						

OYSTER LADLES.—Threaded Handles.

TINNED.

Plain, . . . per dozen,   Pierced, . . . per dozen,

SHALLOW LADLES.—Threaded Handles.

TINNED.

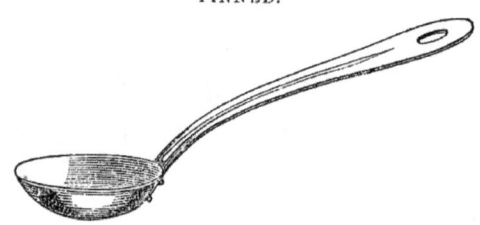

	PLAIN					PIERCED.			
No. . .	1	2	3	4	No. . .	1	2	3	4
Inches, . .	3¼	3½	4	4½	Inches, . .	3¼	3½	4	4½
Per dozen, .					Per dozen,				

SHALLOW LADLES—Wood Handles.

TINNED.

	PLAIN.					PIERCED.			
No. . .	01	02	03	04	No. . .	01	02	03	04
Inches, . .	3¼	3½	4	4½	Inches, . .	3¼	3½	4	4½
Per dozen, . .					Per dozen,				

LADLES.—Patent Threaded.
TINNED.

	PLAIN.						PIERCED.					
No.	14	15	16	17	18	19	14	15	16	17	18	19
Inches,	3¼	3¾	4	4¼	4¾	5½	3¼	3¾	4	4¼	4¾	5½
Per dozen,												

LADLES.—Flat Handles.
TINNED.

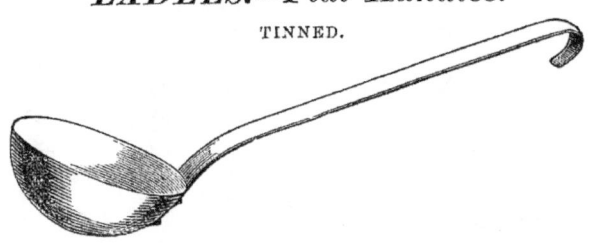

	PLAIN.						PIERCED.					
No.	8	9	10	11	12	13	8	9	10	11	12	13
Inches,	3¼	3¾	4	4¼	4¾	5½	3¼	3¾	4	4¼	4¾	5½
Per dozen,												

LADLES.—Wood Handles.
TINNED.

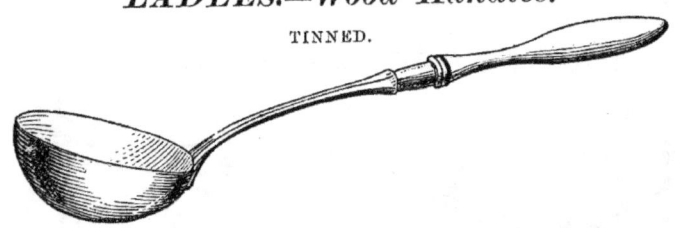

	PLAIN.						PIERCED.					
No.	20	21	22	23	24	25	20	21	22	23	24	25
Inches,	3¼	3¾	4	4¼	4¾	5½	3¼	3¾	4	4¼	4¾	5½
Per dozen,												

LADLES.—Extra Strong.

TINNED.

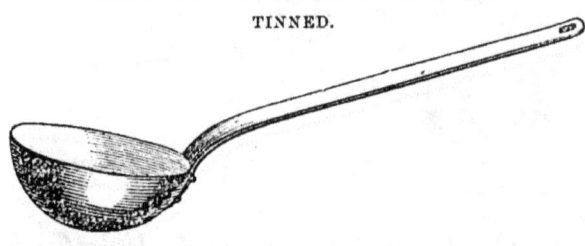

	PLAIN.					PIERCED.			
No.	10	11	12	13	No.	10	11	12	13
Inches,	4	4¼	4¾	5½	Inches,	4	4¼	4¾	5½
Per dozen,					Per dozen,				

NAVY LADLES.

TINNED.

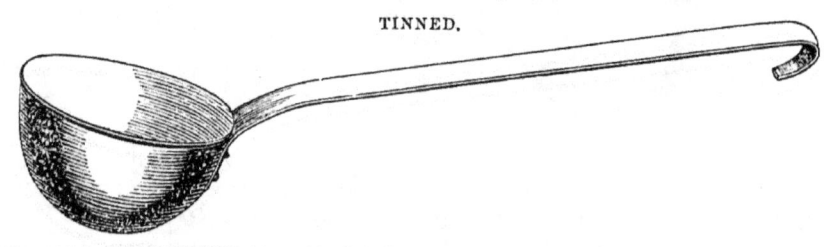

No.	1	2	3	4
Inches,	5½	6		8
Per dozen,				

SOUP LADLES.—Patent Threaded.

TINNED.

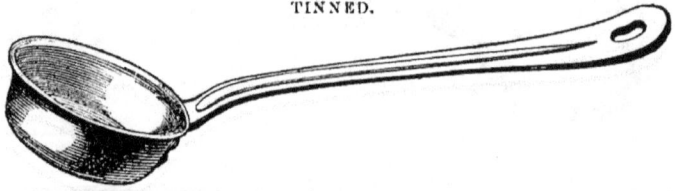

No.	9½	18	19
Inches,	4	3½	3¾
Per dozen,			

SOUP LADLES.—Silver Pattern.

TINNED.

No.	29	30
Inches,	3½	3¾
Per dozen,		

SOUP LADLES.—Wood Handles.

TINNED.

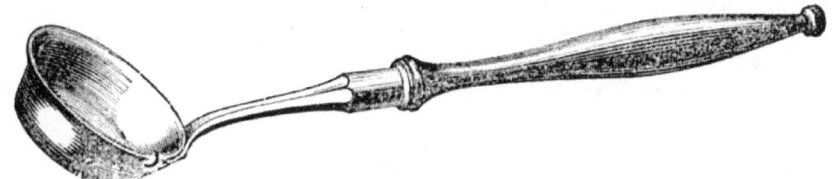

IMITATION OF BRITANNIA.

No.	29	30
Inches,	3½	3¾
Per dozen,		

BRITANNIA SOUP LADLES.—Wood Handles.

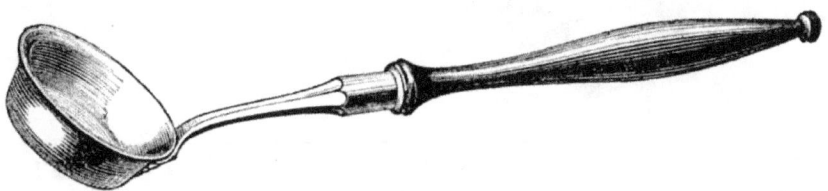

No.	9kkk	9kk	9k	9
Inches,	3	3¼	3½	3¾
Per dozen,				

CUP DIPPERS.—Patent Threaded.

TINNED.

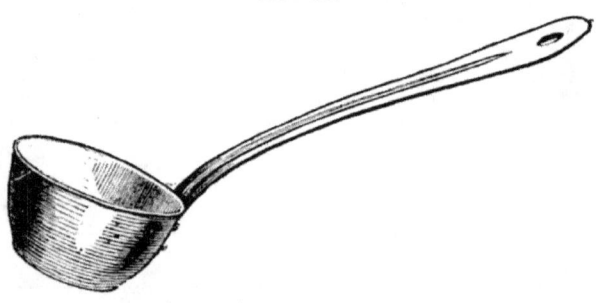

No.	14	15	16	17
Inches,	3¾	4¼	4½	5
Per dozen,				

CUP DIPPERS.—Flat Handles.

TINNED.

No.	8	9	10	11
Inches,	3¾	4¼	4½	5
Per dozen,				

CUP DIPPERS.—Wood Handles.

TINNED.

No.	20	21	22	23
Inches,	3¾	4¼	4½	5
Per dozen,				

FLARING DIPPERS.—Patent Threaded.

TINNED.

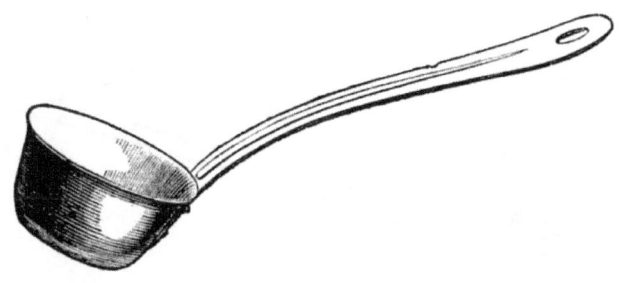

No.	16	17	18	19
Inches,	4¼	4½	4¾	5¼
Per dozen,				

FLARING DIPPERS.—Wood Handles.

TINNED.

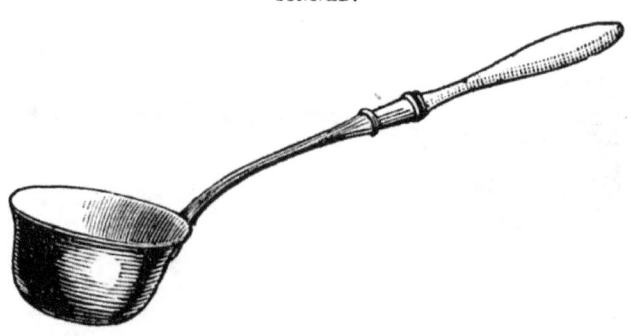

No.	22	23	24	25
Inches,	4¼	4½	4¾	5¼
Per dozen,				

FLAT SKIMMERS.—Flat Handles.

TINNED.

No.	10	11	12	13	14	15
Inches,	4¼	4½	5	5½	5¾	6¼
Per dozen,						

FLESH FORKS.—Two Pronged.

TINNED.

Inches, . .	12	15	18	20	22	24
Per dozen, . . .						

FLESH FORKS.—Three Pronged.

TINNED.

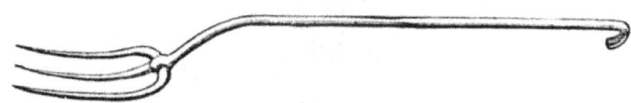

Inches, ...	12	15	18	20	22	24	26
Per dozen, ...							

FLESH FORKS.—Three Pronged.

WOOD HANDLES.

Inches, ...	13	16
Per dozen, ...		

FLESH HOOKS.—Three Pronged.

WOOD HANDLES.

Inches,	13	16
Per dozen,		

MILK SKIMMERS.

TINNED.

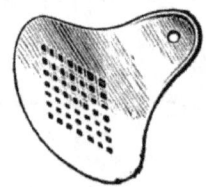

	PLAIN.	PERFORATED.	PLAIN.	PERFORATED.
No.	30	35	Light.	Light.
Inches,	5	5	5	5
Per dozen,				

FRENCH BISCUIT PANS.

TINNED.

Ninety-six to the dozen.

No. 0, ... per dozen,

FRENCH BISCUIT PANS.—Continued.

Ninety-six to the dozen.

No. 00, ... per dozen,

Ninety-six to the dozen.

No. 1, ... per dozen,

FRENCH MUFFIN PANS.
TINNED.

Ninety-six to the dozen.

No. 5, . . per dozen,   *No. 6,* . . per dozen,

FRENCH CORN CAKE PANS.
TINNED.

Ninety-six to the dozen.

No. 4, ... per dozen,

BISCUIT PANS.

TINNED.

No.	10	20	No.	010	020
Inches,	12x8½	15x12	Inches,	12x6	15x8
Per dozen,			Per dozen,		

144 to the dozen.   96 to the dozen.

MUFFIN PANS.

TINNED.

No.	30	40	No.	030	040
Inches,	14x10½	16x12	Inches,	14x7	16x8
Per dozen,			Per dozen,		

144 to the dozen.   96 to the dozen.

CORN CAKE PANS.
TINNED.

No.	50	60	No.	050	060
Inches,	12x9	15x10¼	Inches,	12x6	15x7½
Per dozen,			Per dozen,		

144 to the dozen.   96 to the dozen.

DRINKING CUPS.
TINNED.

	LIGHT.				STRONG.				
No.	08	09	010	011	8	9	10	11	14
Inches,	3¾	4¼	4½	5	3¾	4¼	4½	5	
Per dozen,									

STRAIGHT DRINKING CUPS.
TINNED.

	LIGHT.				STRONG.			
No.	014	015	016	017	No.	14	15	16	17
Inches,	3½	3¾	4	4¼	Inches,	3½	3¾	4	4¼
Per dozen,					Per dozen,				

FAMILY SCOOPS.
TINNED.

FLAT HANDLES.

WOOD HANDLES.

No.	34	35	36	No.	38	39	40
Inches,	4¾	5½	6¼	Inches,	4¾	5½	6¼
Per dozen,				Per dozen,			

GROCER'S SCOOPS.—Metal Handles.
TINNED.

No.	1	2	3	4	5
Inches,		6¾	7¾	9½	11¼
Per dozen,					

GROCER'S SCOOPS.—Wood Handles.
TINNED.

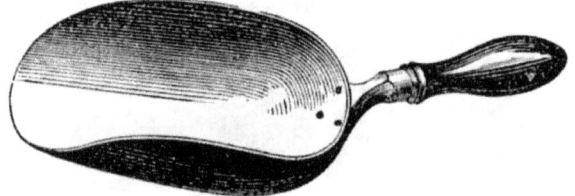

No.	6	7	8	9	10
Inches,		6¾	7¾	9½	11¼
Per dozen,					

COVERED GROCER'S SCOOPS.

TINNED.

METAL HANDLES.

No.	10	20	30	40	50
Inches,		6¾	7¾	9½	11¼
Per dozen,					

COVERED GROCER'S SCOOPS.

TINNED.

WOOD HANDLES.

No.	60	70	80	90	100
Inches,		6¾	7¾	9½	11¼
Per dozen,					

GRAVY STRAINERS.

TINNED.

			WITH FEET	
No.	*5*	*6*	*7*	*8*
Inches,	3¾	4	4¾	5½
Per dozen,				

DINNER KETTLES.

TINNED.

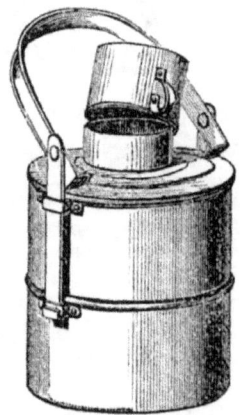  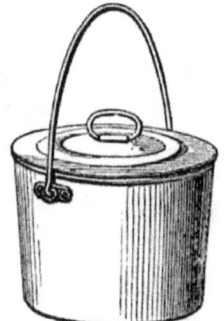

No. 3. *No. 2.* *No. 1.*

No. 1, ... per dozen,
" 2, ... "
" 3, ... "

MUFFIN CUPS.

No.	05	06
Inches, ...	3¼	3¾
Per dozen, ...		

ROUND SIEVES.
TINNED.

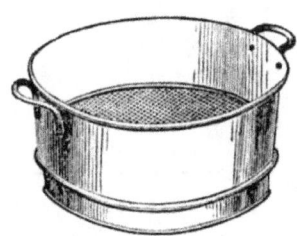

No.	10	12	14	16	18
Inches, ...	4	4¾	5½	6¼	7
Per dozen, . .					

MELTING LADLES.

Inches, ...	2½	3	3½	4	4½	5	5½	6
Per dozen, ...								

TINNERS'

TOOLS AND MACHINES.

Made of the best materials, and all warranted to be in perfect order.

FOLDING MACHINE.

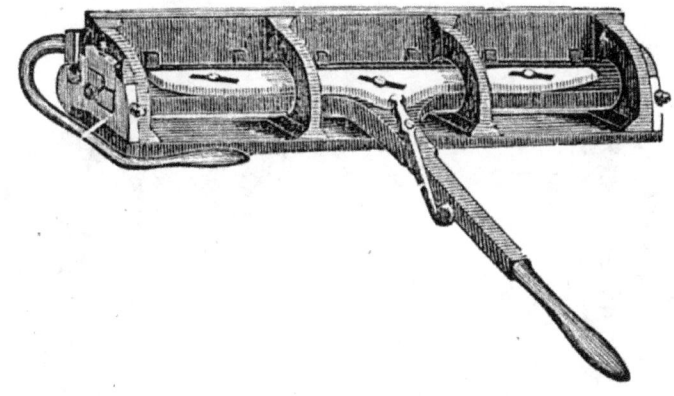

GROOVING MACHINE.

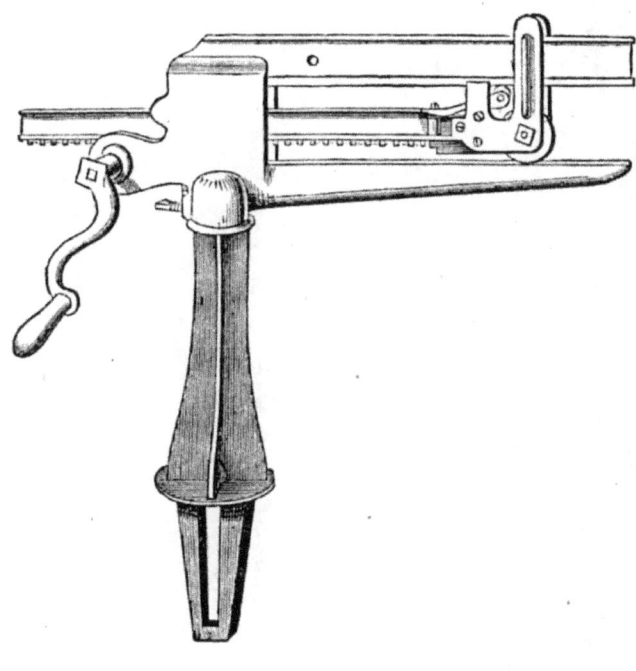

FULL SET No. 1 MACHINES.

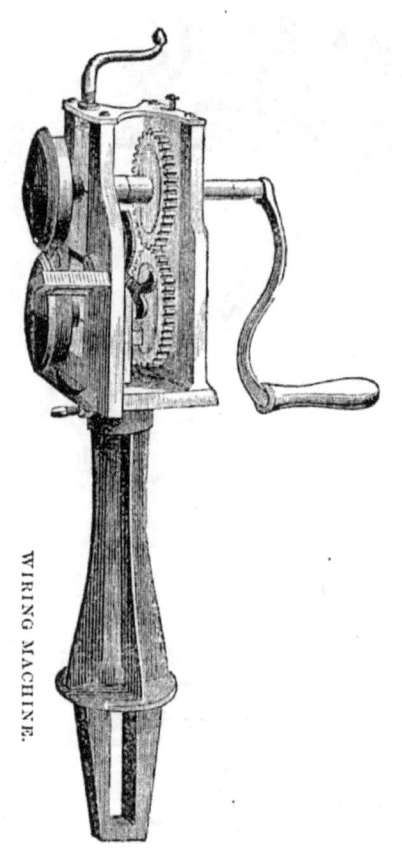

WIRING MACHINE.

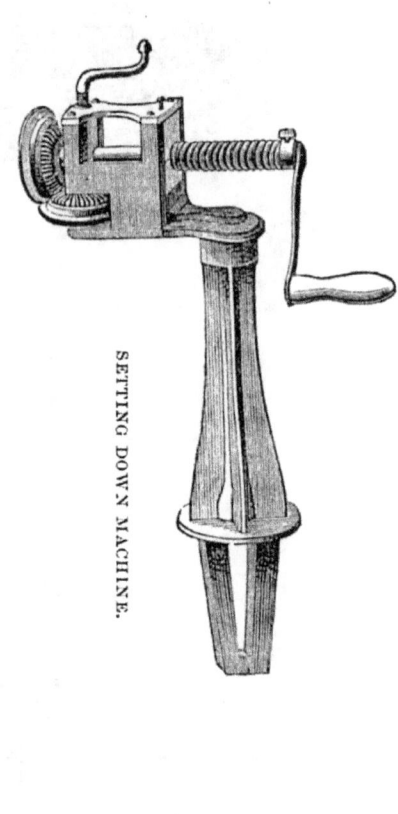

SETTING DOWN MACHINE.

Folding Machine, 17 inch,	$13 50,		$13 50
Grooving " 17 "	9 50,	with Rotary Stand,	10 25
Wiring "	10 75,	" "	11 50
Setting Down "	8 50,	" "	9 25
Large Turning " with Extra Faces,	9 00,	" "	9 75
Small " " " "	8 75,	" "	9 50
Large Burring " " "	7 75,	" "	8 50
Small " " " "	7 25,	" "	8 00
Full Set, without Rotary Stands,	$75 00,	with 7 Rotary Stands,	$80 25
Improved Rotary Standards, each,			75 cts.

FULL SET No. 1 MACHINES.

WITH 20 INCH FOLDER AND GROOVER.

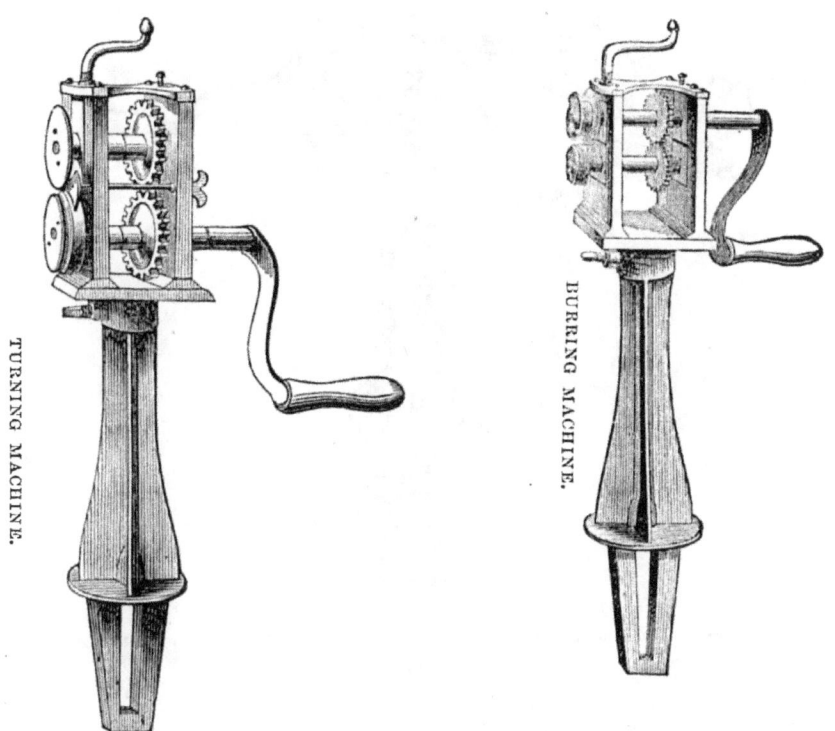

TURNING MACHINE.

BURRING MACHINE.

BRASS WHEELS AND TOP PLATES

Folding Machine, 20 inch,	$18 00
Grooving " 20 " with stand,	12 75
Wiring " "	11 50
Setting Down Machine, "	9 25
Large Turning " "	9 75
Small " " "	9 50
Large Burring " "	8 50
Small " " "	8 00
	$87 25
Improved Rotary Standards, each,	75 cts.

BEADING MACHINES.

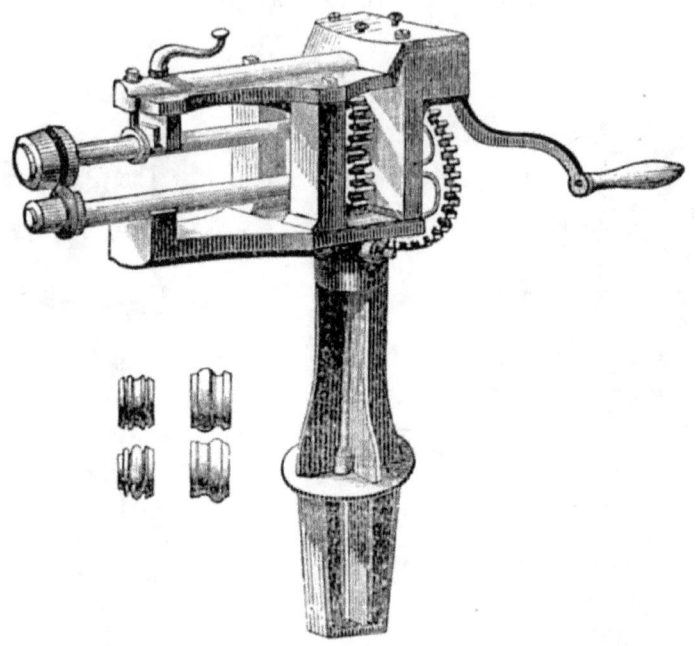

With Wrought Iron Rollers, converted by a new process to Steel, and warranted to be as hard and durable as Cast Steel.

No. 1, Improved, 4 pair Rollers, 13 inch, with Cast Iron Stand,							$34 75
2,	"	4 "	"	10 "	"	"	33 75
3,	"	4 "	"		"	"	28 25
4,	"	4 "	"	for Tin,	"	"	18 75
5,	"	5 "	"	"	"	"	15 75
Extra Wrought Iron Rollers, per pair, to No. 1 and 2,							3 50
"	"	"	"	No. 3,			3 00
"	"	"	"	No. 4,			2 00
"	"	"	"	No. 5,			1 25
Standards for Nos. 1, 2 and 3, each,							1 25
"	"	4 and 5, each,					75

The impressions given are $1\frac{1}{8}$ inch, 1 inch, $\frac{7}{8}$ inch, $\frac{1}{2}$ round, O. G. Coffee Pot, Cullender, Elbow, Astragal, and any other form required.

The improved Beading Machine brings the work towards the operator. The Common Beaders carry it from him.

FORMING MACHINES.

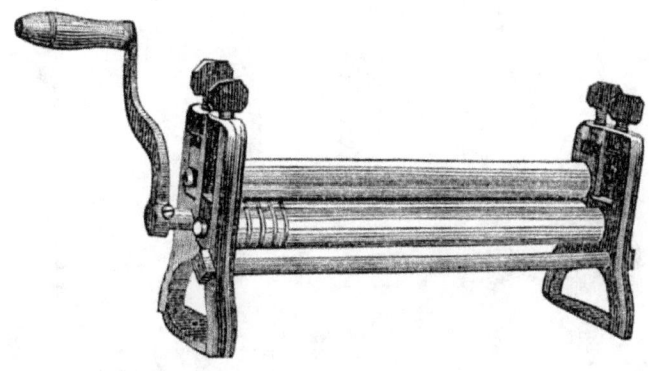

TIN PIPE FORMER.

No. 00, Extra Large for heavy Plate, Double Geared, 3 inch Rolls, 37 inches long,		$60 00
No. 0, for Cans, &c., 2 inch Rolls, 37 inches long,		24 00
1, Stove Pipe, 2 " 30 "		19 00
2, " 1¾ " 30 "		18 00
1, Tin Pipe, 1½ " 20 "		10 00
2, " 1½ " 16 "		9 00
Blacking, Pepper, or Rattle-Box and Candlestick Former and Beader, Steel Rods,		18 00
Candle Mould and Dipper Handle Former,		16 00
" " Tip Former,		15 00
Jacket Lamp Former,		20 00
Canister Top "		20 00
Iron Frame for Stove Pipe,		5 00

Extra Formers to order.

VALENTINE'S
PATENT UNIVERSAL TUBE FORMER.

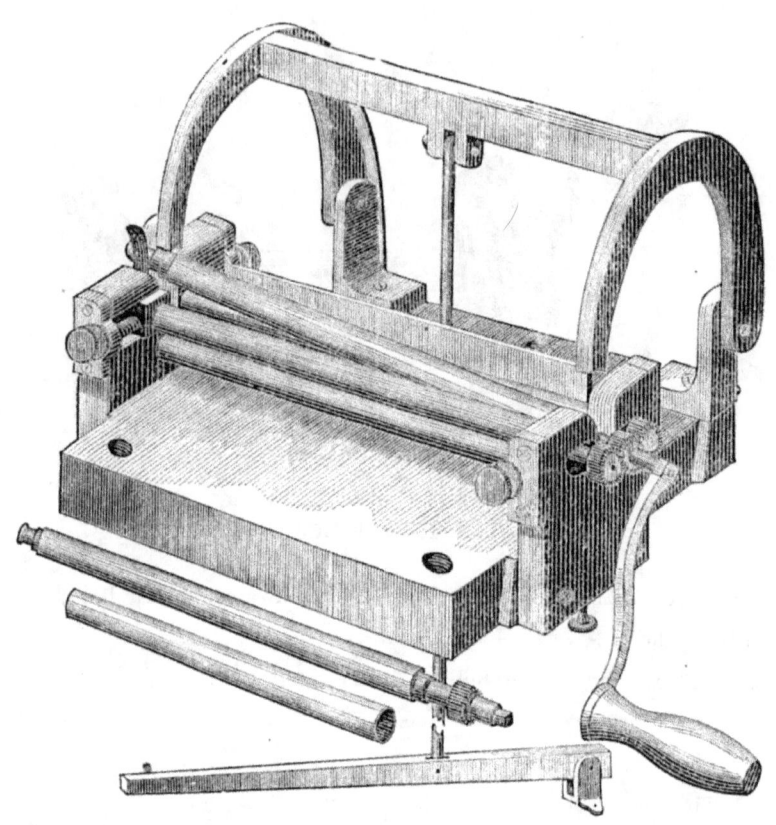

For Candle Moulds, or Ladle Handles, 11 inches long, ... $25 00
Extra Rollers, per set, ...

STOW'S PATENT TUBE FORMERS.

No. 00, To form Speaking Tubes, 24 inches long, ... $50 00
    0, To form Tubes, 15 inches long, ... 24 00
    1, For Candle Moulds or Ladle Handles, 11 inches long, ... 20 00
    2, For Tea Kettle Spouts, &c., 8 inches long, ... 18 00
    3, For Rattle-Box Handles, 5 inches long, ... 16 00
    4, For Lamp Tubes, 2½ inches long, ... 15 00
Additional Die Rods and Beds, extra.

O. W. STOW'S PATENT FOLDING MACHINE, No. 1.

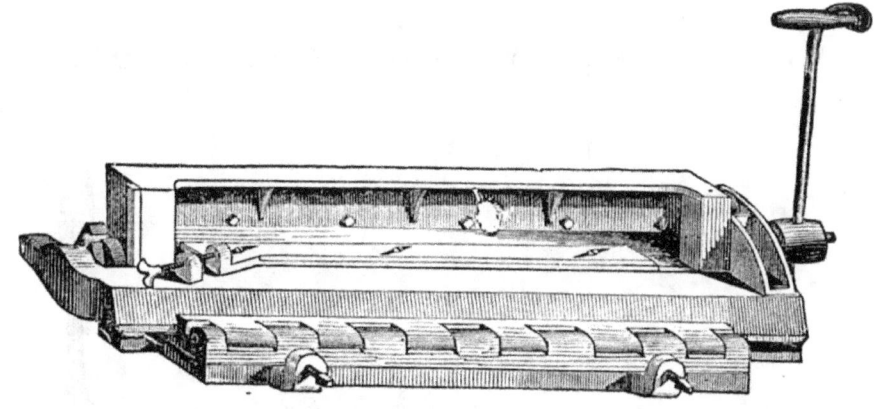

TIN FOLDING MACHINES.

No. 00, O. W. Stow's Patent,			17 inches,	. . . .	$13 50
0,	"	"	"	20	"	18 00
1,	"	"	"	22	"	20 00
2,	"	"	"	17	"	15 00
1, Whitney's,				22	"	20 00
2,	"			17	"	15 00
Large, Old style,				20	"	18 00
Small,	"			17	"	13 50
No. 1, Walker's Patent,				20	"	18 00
2,	"	"		17	"	14 00

Wood Bottom Sheet Iron Folding Machine.

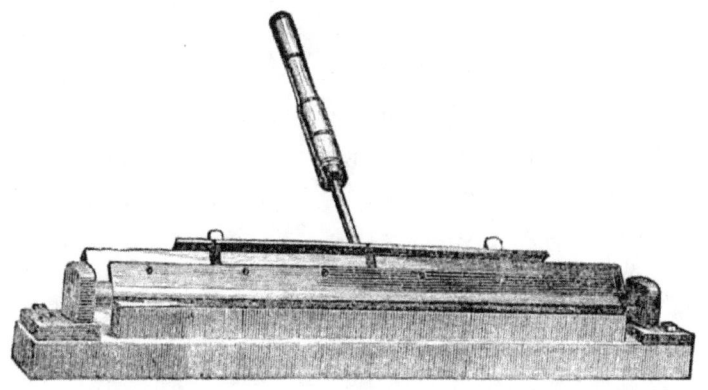

WRIGHT'S PATENT SHEET IRON FOLDER.

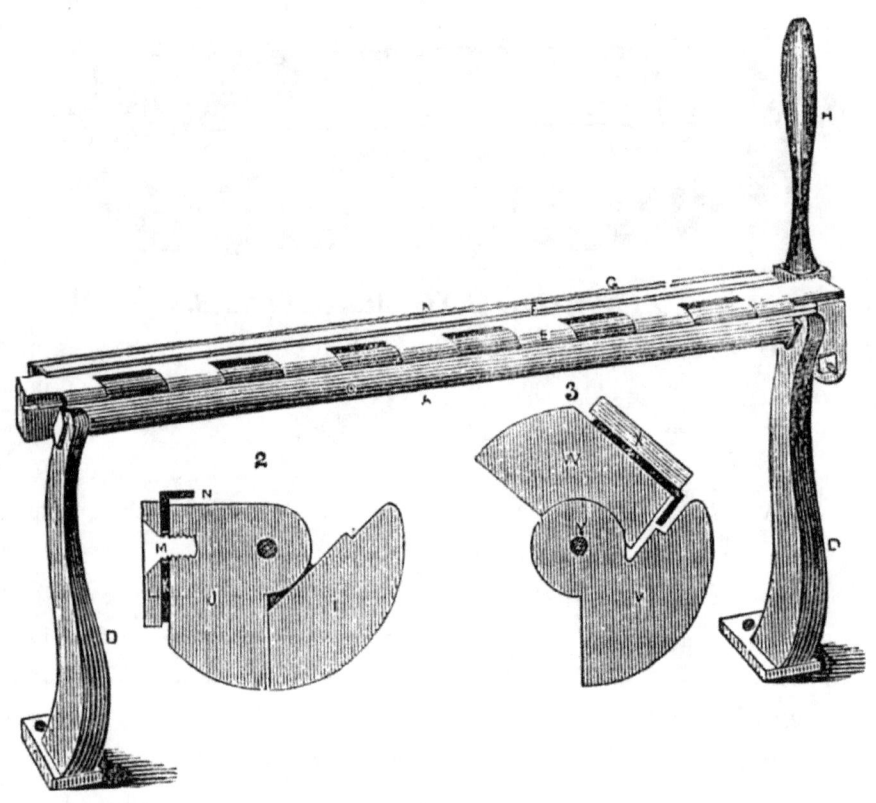

No.	0, Wood Bottom, Sheet Iron,	48 inches,	$16 00
	1, " " "	30 "	10 00
	2, Iron " "	30 "	6 50
	3, " " "	39 "	10 00
	000, Wright's Patent, "	11 feet,	120 00
	0, " " "	3½ "	15 00
	1, " " "	2½ "	10 00
	2, " " for Tin,	20 inches,	8 00

O. W. STOW'S IMPROVED GUTTER BEADER.

No. 3, IRON BOTTOM GUTTER BEADER.

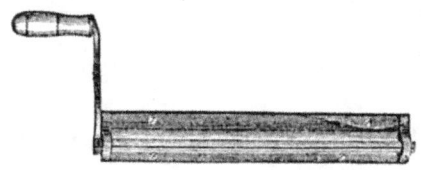

GUTTER MACHINES.

No. 0, with 2 Wood Rolls, ⅜ Cast Steel Rod, 20 inches,					. . . .	$5 00
1, with 2 " " ⅝ " " 15 "					. . . .	4 50
2, Iron Bottom, ⅜ or ½ " " 20 "					. . . .	4 00
3, " ⅜ or ½ " " 15 "					. . . .	3 50
1, O. W. Stow's Improved, 20 "					. . . .	5 50
2, " " " 15 "					. . . .	4 50
1, Enclosed Cast Steel Rod, 5-16, ⅜ or ½ inch, 20 inches,					. . . .	4 00
2, " " " 5-16, ⅜ or ½ " 15 "					. . . .	3 50
1, Epply's Patent Cast Steel Rod, 15 "					. . . .	3 50
1, Gutter Rods, Extra, 20 "					. . . .	2 25
2, " " " 15 "					. . . .	2 00

BIGELOW'S PATENT GROOVER.

FOR TIN OR SHEET IRON.

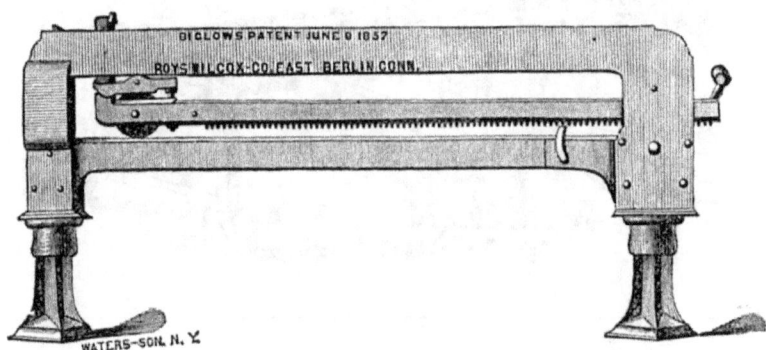

Works 30 inches,	$32 00
Stands, each,	1 25

WALKER'S PATENT TIN FOLDER.

No. 1, Machine, 20 inches,	$18 00
2, " 17 "	14 00

SHEPARD & STOW'S
PATENT WIRING MACHINE.

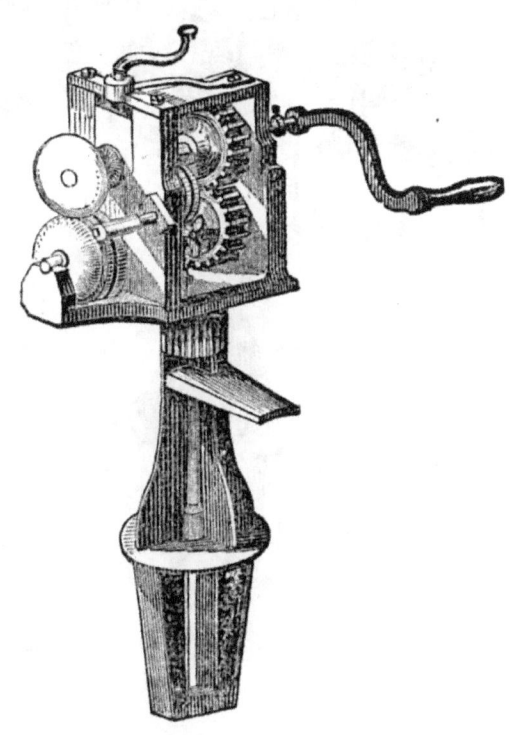

SUNDRY MACHINES.

No. 0, Wiring by Steam or Hand power, for Brass Kettles, &c., Shepard & Stow's Patent, ...	$50 00
No. 1, Wiring, Shepard & Stow's Patent, with Standard, ...	15 00
2, " " " " " "	13 75
Wiring, for Brass Kettles and other heavy work by Steam or Hand power,	25 00
Standard, for do., ...	1 25
Large Turning, for Brass Kettles and other heavy work by Steam or Hand,	25 00
Standard, for do., ...	1 25
Bigelow's Patent Sheet Iron Grooving Machine, 30 inches, ...	32 00
Large Grooving for 20 inch Tin, with Rotary Standard, ...	12 75

CRIMPING MACHINE.

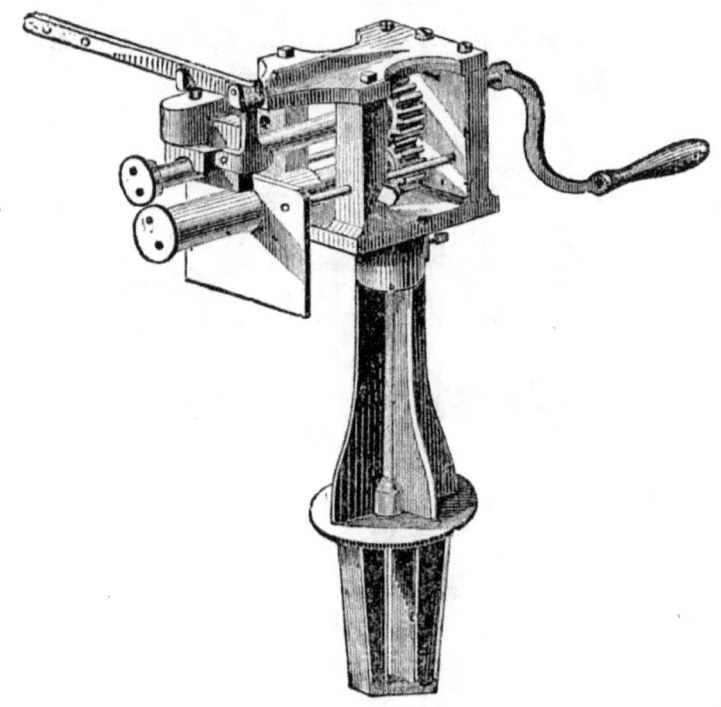

SUNDRY MACHINES.—Continued.

No. 1, Crimping, for putting Tops and Bottoms on Boxes, Cans, Cups, &c., with Standard,	14 75
No. 2, Crimping, for similar purposes, with Standard,	12 75
Flanging, for Burring inside of Rim,	15 00
Contracting, for connecting Stove Pipe, No. 1,	18 00
Iron Standard, for do.,	1 25
Contracting, for connecting Stove Pipe, No. 2,	10 00
Iron Standard, for do.,	75
Elbow, for Stove Pipe, &c.,	8 00
Iron Standard, for do.,	75
Pepper-Box or Extra small Burr,	7 50
Iron Standard, for do.,	75
Wire Spring Former, (or Winder,)	3 00

BURTON'S DOUBLE SEAMER.

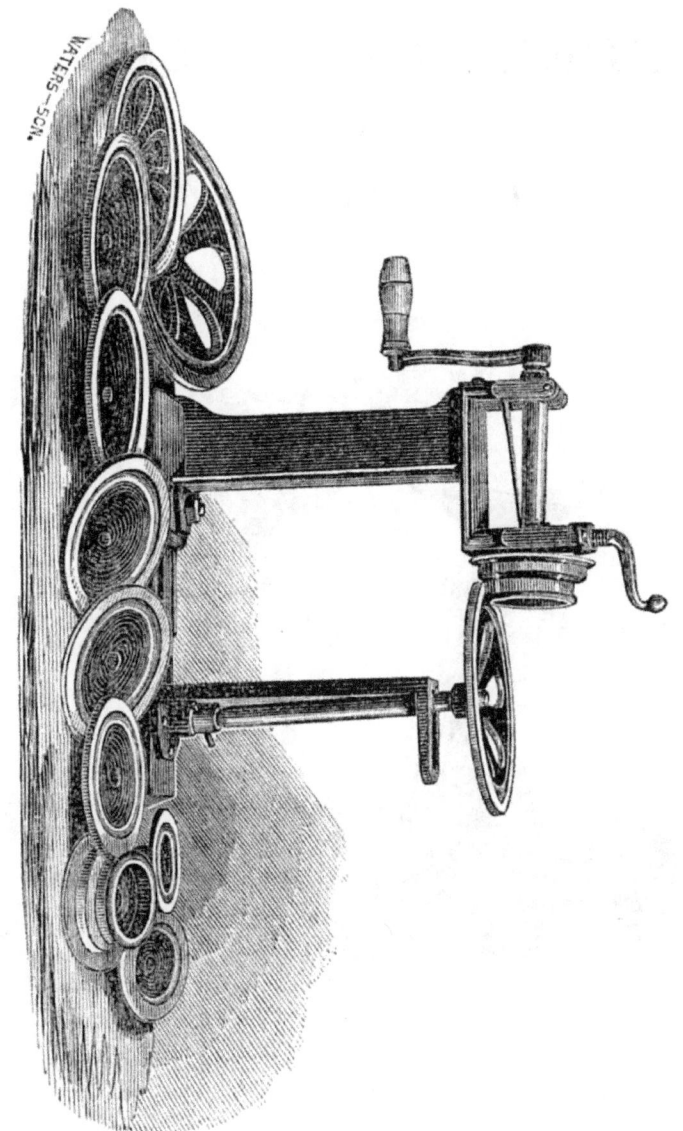

Burton's Patent Double Seamer, ... $21 00

OLMSTED'S
PATENT DOUBLE SEAMER

AND

SETTING DOWN MACHINE COMBINED.

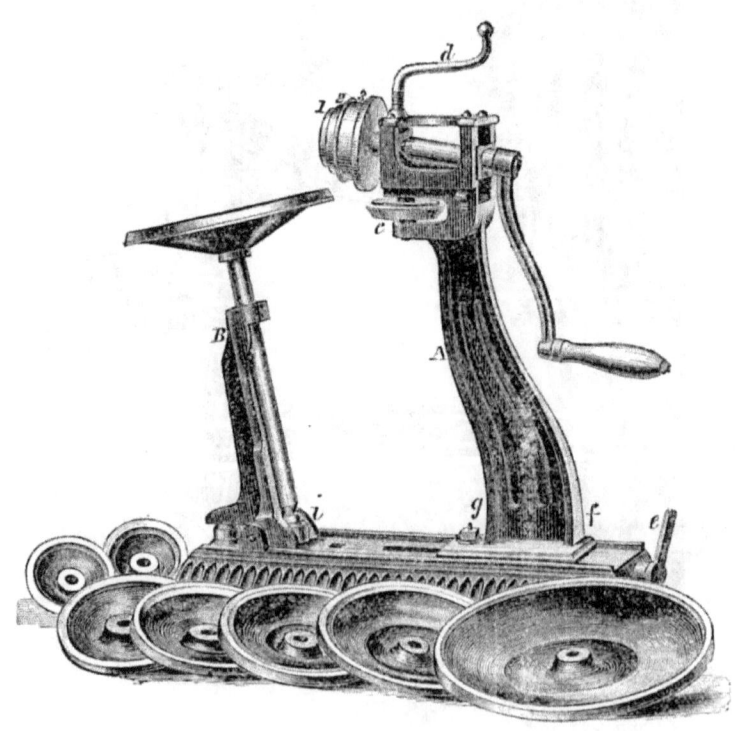

EIGHT PAIR OF DISCS.

No. 1, ... $45 00

[FOR DIRECTIONS SEE OPPOSITE PAGE.]

DIRECTIONS.

Place the machine on a solid bench—make it firm and oil well.

In setting the machine for use:

1st. Place the disc of the required size on the Spindle, and bring the standard B perpendicular to the base; then shove the standard A toward the disc until the Setting Down Wheel surely touches the disc, remembering always when the machine is set for use, to have the disc at least one-sixteenth or one-eighth of an inch above the Setting Down Wheel c, which is raised or lowered, as the thickness of the Tin requires, by means of a screw in the bottom of the Stepping, raising on the eccentric underneath the base at i. Having made the standard A fast to the base with the bolt at the bottom, the machine is ready for operation.

2d. When the machine is set for Setting Down work, it is also set for Double Seaming; simply turning the lever toward you, as far as it will go, changes the machine to Double Seaming.

3d. When the machine is Setting Down work, let the hand lie upon the Tin very lightly.

4th. In Double Seaming never shove the Tin with the hand, in order to urge or help the machine; if anything, place one hand on the outer edge of the Tin, and pull the work gently back. By observing this, work can be Double Seamed, the diameter of which is much larger than the disc itself.

5th. The machine will Set Down and Double Seam the most difficult kind of work, *tight* or *loose* bottoms, even without the assistance of the hand.

6th. Section 1, is for Double Seaming raised work; section 2, for straight work and coffee pots; and section 3, for flaring work.

7th. To Deflect Straight work run it through section 3, either before or after Double Seaming; if before, it will turn the seam down more than halfway, when it can be closed up with section 2.

8th. To Double Seam flaring work without Deflecting, (which can be done at the same time if desired,) detach sections 1 and 2 with a wrench.

9th. All deflected bottoms will not spring when soldered, and in order to take the spring out of non-deflected bottoms run them through the machine after soldering.

10th. Flaring work is seamed upon flaring discs; straight work upon straight discs. Flaring work *can* be seamed on straight discs.

11th. In using the machine on 2, 3 and 4 Cross Tin, by placing a strip of tin underneath that side of standard A, from you, at g and f, it will work much easier and thereby save power—though it will accomplish the same object without—but turn harder.

12th. The pressure sufficient to turn the seams upon the different grades of Tin is regulated by the screw d.

☞ By observing the foregoing directions in the use of the Olmsted Machine, any one not a practical tinner may use it with accuracy and dispatch.

MOORE'S PATENT DOUBLE SEAMERS.

Moore's Patent,	No. 1, for Heavy Metal,	$21 00
"	" No. 2, for Common Work,	19 00
"	" No. 3, for " "	19 00

SQUARE BOX FOLDING MACHINE.

Square Box Folding Machine, 20 inch, worked by foot, accurate and expeditious in its operations, ... $20 00
Box Former and Beader, ... 20 00

WIRE WINDER.

TEA KETTLE STAKE.

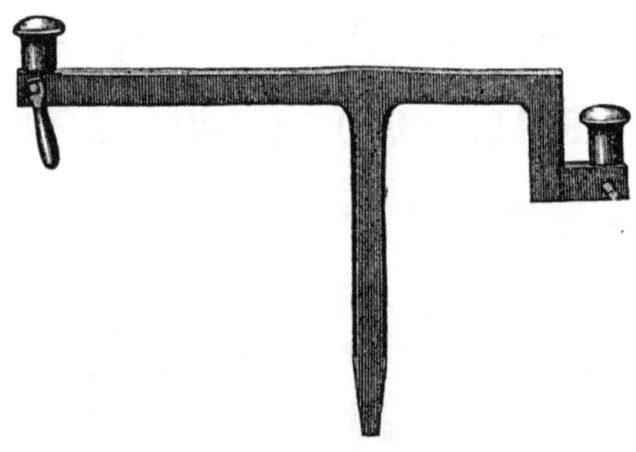

Tea Kettle Stake, Wrought Iron Standard, ... $8 75
Extra Heads for Tea Kettle Stake, Cast Steel, each, ...   1 75

BENCH PLATES.

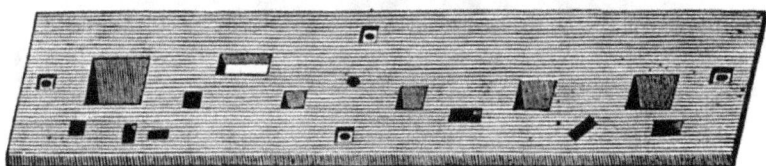

No. 1, ... $5 00
" 2, ...   3 00

SQUARE PAN TURNER.

No. 1, 20 inch Steel, ... $2 50
" 2, 15 "   " 2 00

ROYS & WILCOX CO'S
PATTERN SQUARING SHEARS,

FOR CUTTING SHEET METALS, PAPER, &C.

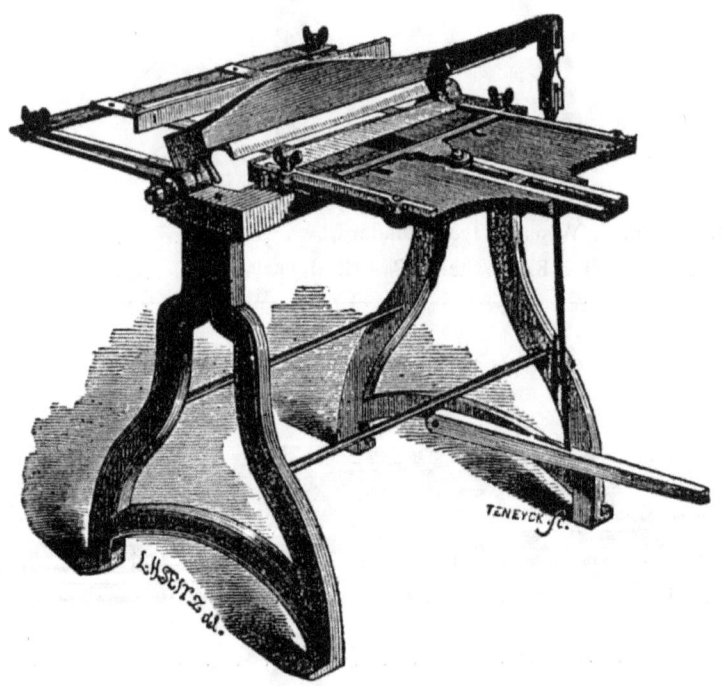

A GREAT LABOR-SAVING MACHINE.

No. 00, R. & W. Co. Pattern with iron frame, cut 37 inches,		$125 00
" 0, " " " " " " 30 "		120 00
" 1, R. & W., or P. S. Co. Pattern, with iron frame, cut 30 inches,		47 00
" 1, " " " " without " " 30 "		40 00
" 2, " " " " with " " 20 "		32 00
" 2, " " " " without " " 20 "		26 00
Extra Blades, No. 2, per pair, ...		9 00
" " No. 1, "		12 00
" " No. 0 & 00, "		16 00

Lever Shears of any desired length, (for cutting straight work,) made to order.

STOW'S PATTERN SQUARING SHEARS.

FOR CUTTING SHEET METALS, &C.

These Shears are arranged with Gauges for squaring, stripping and cutting at any desired angle, without the necessity of marking the sheet, and doing the work much quicker.

No. 0, are for cutting Sheets (30 inches) of Heavy Metal, Steel, Iron, Brass or Copper.

No. 1, are for cutting Sheet Iron, &c. No. 2, for Tin and other light metals.

No. 1, Stow's Pattern, with iron frame, cut 30 inches,	$50 00
" 2, " " " " " 20 "	35 00
Extra Blades, No. 2, per pair,	9 00
" " No. 1, "	12 00
" " No. 0 & 00, "	16 00

ROTARY SHEARS.

Savage's Patent Improved.

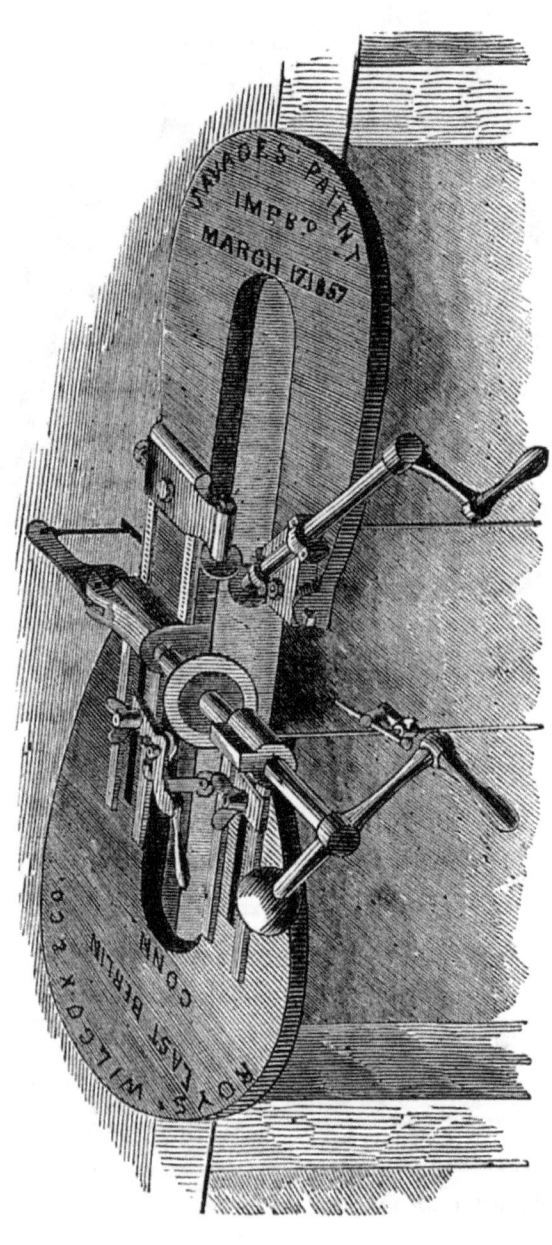

SAVAGE'S PATENT

IMPROVED

COMBINATION ROTARY SHEARS,

WITH BURRING ATTACHMENT OR EDGE TURNER.

For which Premiums have been awarded by the Crystal Palace Association and the American Institute, New York.

The manufacturers inform the Workers and Dealers in Tin Plate, that after many years experimenting, they have succeeded, at large expense, in obtaining a Machine that will cut Circles from Tin and bend (or burr) the same at any desired angle, without extra discs; or with a small additional expense, can be used for bending (or turning) edges at right angles, being more than any other Machine ever invented is capable of doing.

No. 0, For Heavy Metal, with Burring Attachment,	$160 00
Extra Disc, per pair, not over 12 inches diameter,	9 00
" Cutters, per pair,	3 50
No. 1, For Light Metal, with Burring Attachment,	35 00
" " " " without " "	30 00
Extra Discs, (not exceeding 8 inches diameter,) or cutters, per pair,	1 50
" Cutter Stocks, per pair,	2 50
Large Rotary Shears, to go by Steam or Water Power, made in a superior manner, expressly for trimming Boiler Bottoms and Brass Kettles, Oval or Round,	220 00
Low's Patent Shears, for cutting parallel curves for Pan sections, &c.,	80 00
Low's Beveling " " " ends of Pan sections, &c.,	45 00

FLANDER'S PATENT
IMPROVED
CIRCULAR OR ROTARY SHEARS,

FOR CUTTING AND BENDING.

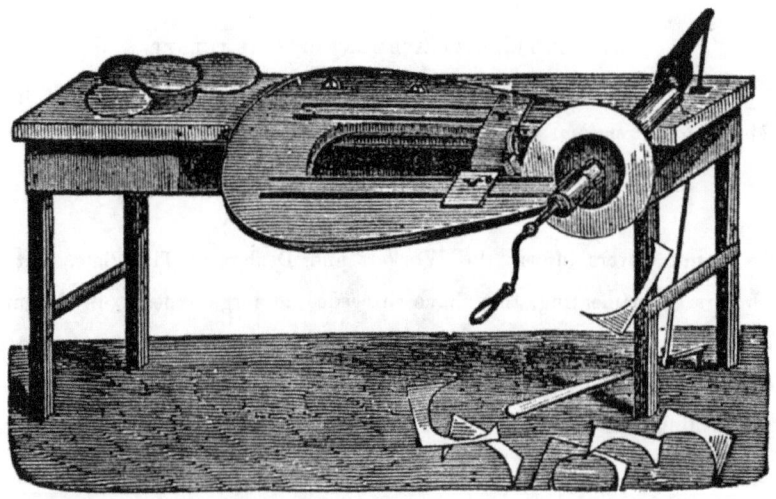

For which a Gold Medal was awarded by the American Institute of New York, a Medal and Diploma by the Massachusetts Charitable Mechanic Association, and a Medal and Diploma by the Exhibition of the Industry of all Nations at the Crystal Palace, New York, 1853.

No. 0, Operated by Steam or Hand Power, for Gas Metres, &c., with 1 pair 10¼ inch Disc, and 1 pair Cutters on Iron Frame,	$140 00
Extra Discs, (average,) per pair,	9 00
Extra Cutters,	3 50
No. 1, Operated by Hand, for Tin, &c., with 4 pair Discs, 1 pair Cutters and Edge Turner,	30 00
No. 1, Without Edge Turner,	25 00
Extra Discs, (not exceeding 8 inches diameter,) or Cutters, per pair,	1 50
Extra Cutter, Stocks, per pair,	2 50

Creasing Swedge.

Cullender Swedge.

Square Pan Swedge.

SWEDGES.

Creasing,	$5 25	Square Pan,	$5 00
Cullender,	4 75	Elbow,	5 00

Blowhorn Stake.

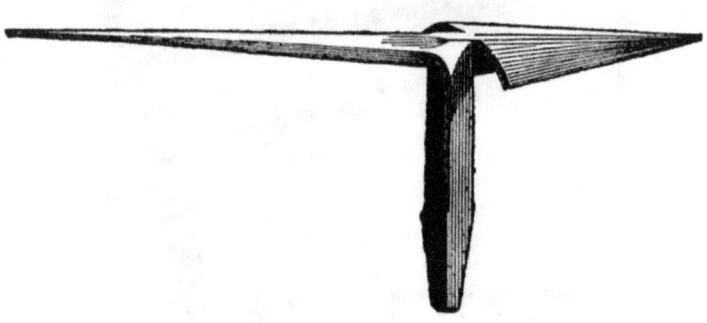

Creasing Stake.

Square Stake.

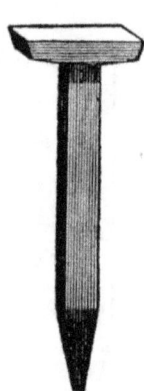

Candle Mould Stake.

Needle Case Stake.

BEAK HORN STAKE.

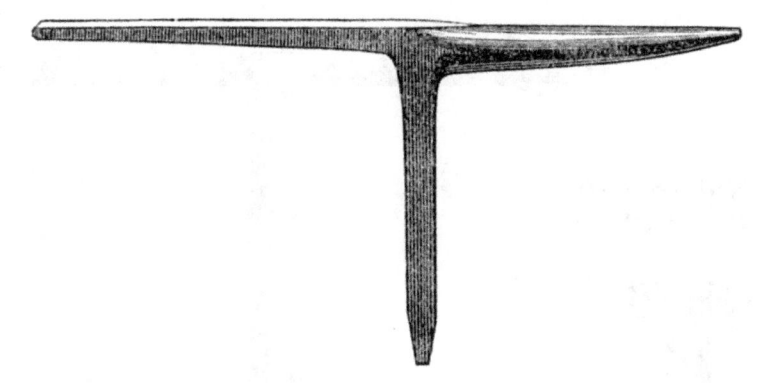

TOOLS.—Articles included in the Set.

1 Large Stake, (or Beak Horn,) No. 1,	$15 00
1 Blowhorn, "	5 00
1 Creasing, "	4 00
1 Square, "	3 00
1 Candle Mould, "	2 75
1 Needle Case, "	2 25
1 Set Hollow Punches—each ½, ¾, 1, 1½, 1¾ inch,	5 50
1 Set Solid " (4 Punches and 2 Chisels,)	0 72
1 Creasing Swedge,	5 25
1 Cullender Swedge,	4 75
1 Pair Shears, No. 4,	5 50
1 Raising Hammer, each No. 1 and 4,	3 00
1 Setting " " No. 2 and 3,	1 00
1 Riveting " No. 5,	0 28
The above comprise a full set,	$58 00

IMPROVED CUTTING NIPPERS.

No. 1, Extra Large Size,	$2 25
" 2, Large Size,	2 00
" 3, Common Size,	1 50
" 4, Small "	1 40
" 5, " "	1 00

Double Seaming Stake.

Coppersmith Square Stake.

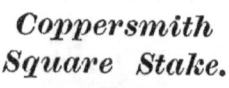
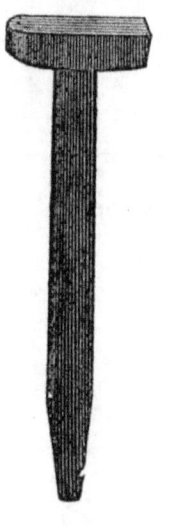

Hatchet Stake.

Bottom Stake.

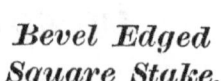

Bevel Edged Square Stake.

STAKES.

No. 1, Large (or Beak Horn,) 45 lbs.,	$15 00
" 2, " " 40 "	13 25
" 3, " " 35 "	11 50
" 4, " " 30 "	10 00
" 1, Double Seaming, large end 16 inches, small end 11 inches,	9 00
" 2, " " each end 11 inches,	8 00
" 0, Conductor, each end 14 inches,	6 00
" 1, Bevel, Edged Square,	6 00
" 2, " " "	5 00
Common Blowhorn,	5 00
Creasing with horn,	4 50
Common Creasing,	4 00
Coppersmith Square,	3 50
Common "	3 00
Candle Mould,	2 75
Needle Case,	2 25
Small Square,	1 25
Tea Kettle, Wrought Iron Standard,	8 75
Heads for Tea Kettle, each, Cast Steel,	1 75
No. 1, HATCHET, blade 16 inches long,	5 00
" 2, " " 14½ "	4 25
" 3, " " 13 "	3 50
" 4, " " 11 "	2 75
" 5, " " 9 "	2 25
" 6, " " 7 "	1 75
" 1, BOTTOM, Width 1¾ "	75
" 2, " " 1½ "	63
" 3, " " 1¼ "	50
" 4, " " 1 "	37

Conductor Stake.

Mandrel Stake.

Double Seaming Stake with 4 Heads.

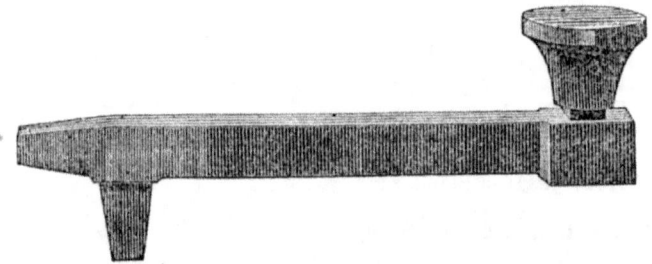

Extra Heads for 4 Head Stake.

Round Head Stake.

STAKES.—Continued.

CAST IRON.

No. 1, Conductor, Turned,				$ 4 00
" 2, " "				3 00
" 00, Mandrel, 5 feet long,				10 00
" 0, " 3 feet 4 inches,				6 00
" 1, " 2 " 10 "				5 00
" 2, " 2 " 6 "				4 00
" 3, " 2 " 3 "				3 00
Hollow "				5 50
Grooving "				5 50
Boiler "				5 00
Double Seaming, with 4 Heads,				9 00
Extra Heads for Double Seaming,				1 50
Common Double Seaming,				5 00
Bevel Edged Square,				2 50
Round Head,				1 25
Candle Mould Square,				75
Bath Tub,				1 25

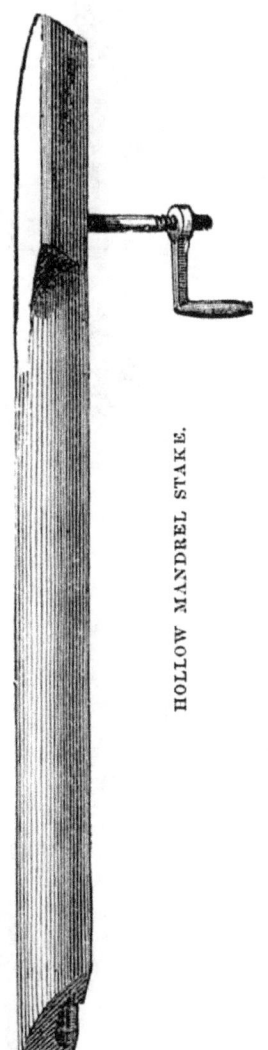

HOLLOW MANDREL STAKE.

Bath Tub Stake.

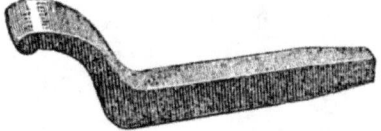

ROOFING TONGS:

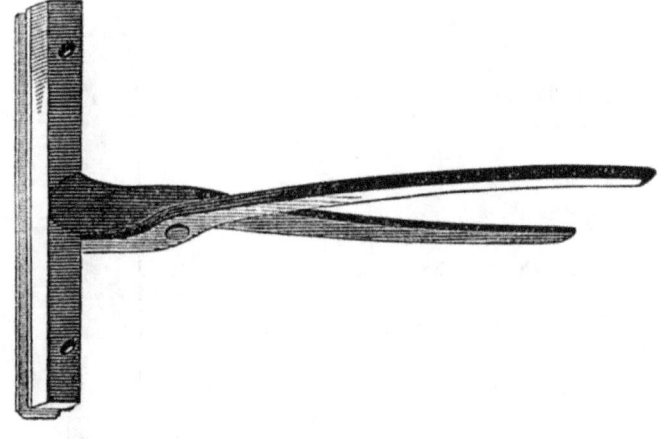

ROOFING DOUBLE SEAMER.

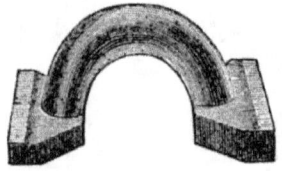

WOOD ROOFING FOLDER.

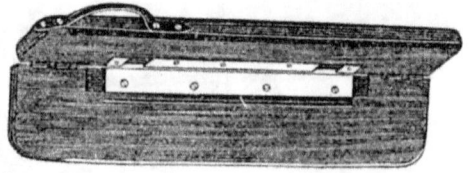

ROOFING TOOLS.

Roofing Tongs, (Steel,) per set, 2 pairs,	$6 00
Roofing Double Seamers, " 2 pieces,	1 75
Roofing Folder, improved, 20 inch. Iron,	5 00
Roofing Folder, " Wood,	3 00
Gutter Tongs, each,	5 00

BENCH SHEARS.

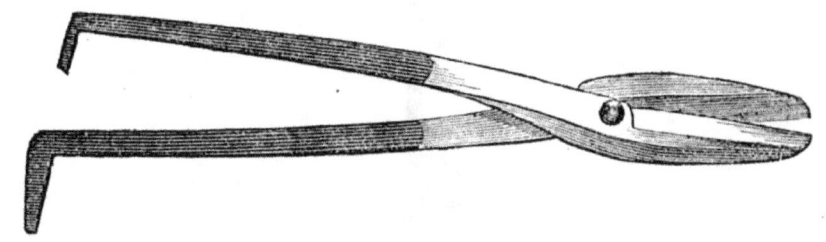

SHEARS.

No. 00,	Bench Cut,	12	inches,		$13 50
" 0,	"	"	10½	"	12 00
" 1,	"	"	9	"	9 00
" 2,	"	"	8⅝	"	8 00
" 3,	"	"	8⅜	"	6 50
" 4,	"	"	8	"	5 50
" 5,	"	"	7	"	4 50
" 6,	"	"	6	"	3 50
" 6½	Hand Cut,		4½	"	3 25
" 7,	"	"	4	"	2 75
" 8,	"	"	3½	"	2 25
" 9,	"	"	3	"	1 75
" 10,	"	"	2½	"	1 50
Circular	"	No. 9,			2 50
"	"	No. 8,			3 00
"		No. 7,			3 50
Elbow Bench,					5 25
Band Box Bench,					6 00

HAND SHEARS.

HOLLOW PUNCHES.

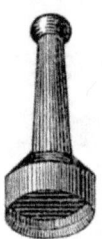

All sizes to and including 1¾ inch diameter, Round, per inch, ... $1 00
All sizes above 1¾ inch diameter, Round, per inch, ... 1 25
Oval, per inch, ... 1 50

Wilcox's Pattern.

All sizes to and including 1⅜ inch diameter, per inch, ... $1 00
All sizes above 1⅜ inch diameter, per inch, ... 75

SET SOLID PUNCHES.

Square, C. S., No. 0, 1, 2, 3, 4, 5, 6, 7, 8 and Prick, each, ... $0 12
Round Steel, ... 10

CAST STEEL CHISELS.

Circular, per inch, ... $0 25
Lantern, Common Size, ... 12
Wire, ... ¼—½—⅝—¾—⅞—1—1⅛—1¼—1½—1¾—2 inch.
                                       8 10 11 12 13 14 15 17 20 24 29 cts.

RIVET SET AND HEADERS.

Nos. 00 and 0, C. S., extra, each,	$0 75
" 1 and 2, " " "	63
" 3 and 4, " " "	50
" 5 and 6, " " "	37
" 7 and 8, " " "	31
Ornament Sets, " " "	37

GROOVING TOOLS.

Nos. 00 and 0, each,	$0 75
" 1 and 2, "	63
" 3 and 4, "	50
" 5 and 6, "	37
" 7 and 8, "	25

HAMMERS.

No. 1, Raising,	$2 25
" 2, "	1 75
" 3, "	1 25
" 4, "	75
Extra Handles, per dozen,	1 00

HAMMERS.—Continued.

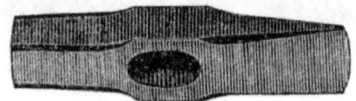

							With Handle.
No. 0, Riveting,	Heavy Work, Bright,	1½ inch,		$0 87,		$0 97
" 1, "	Sheet Iron, "	C. S., 1⅛ inch,		75,		85
" 2, "	Tin, &c., "	1 "		63,		73
" 3, "	" "	⅞ "		50,		60
" 4, "	" "	¾ "		38,		48
" 5, "	" "	⅝ "		33,		43
" 0, "	Heavy Work, Black,	1½ "		75,		85
" 1, "	Sheet Iron, "	1⅛ "		69,		79
" 2, "	Tin, &c., "	1 "		56,		66
" 3, "	" "	⅞ "		44,		54
" 4, "	" "	¾ "		32,		42
" 5, "	" "	⅝ "		28,		38

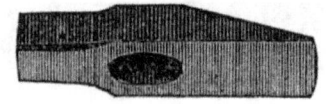

					With Handle.
No. 1, Setting, Bright, C. S., 1⅛ inch,		$0 75,		$0 85
" 2, " " " 1 "		63,		73
" 3, " " " ⅞ "		50,		60
" 4, " " " ¾ "		38,		48
" 5, " " " ⅝ "		33,		43
" 1, " Black, 1⅛ "		69,		79
" 2, " " 1 "		56,		66
" 3, " " ⅞ "		44,		54
" 4, " " ¾ "		32,		42
" 5, " " ⅝ "		28,		38

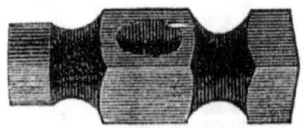

Planishing, per pound,	$1 00
Cast Iron Raising, No. 1,	1 00
" " " 2,	75
" " " 3,	50
" " " 4,	38
Handles, per dozen, extra,	1 00

PLUMBERS' SCRAPERS.

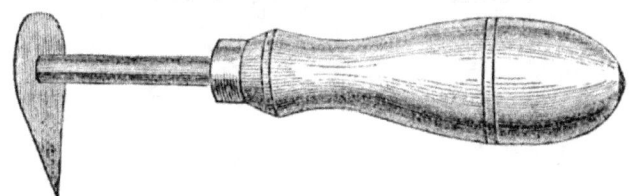

No. 1, ... per dozen,

GEARED DRILLS.

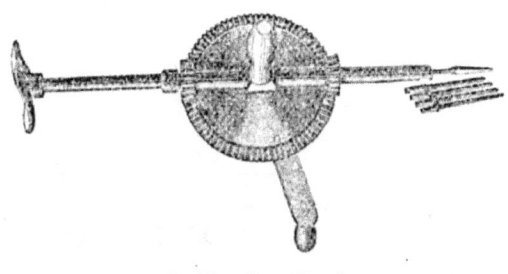

No. 1, Double Geared Stocks, 4 Drills, Cast Steel, each, ... $3 50
" 2, Single   "   " 4   "   "   " 2 00
" 3,   "   "   "   Common, "   " 1 75

COLD CHISELS.

Octagon Cast Steel, ... $\frac{3}{8}$ — $\frac{1}{2}$ — $\frac{5}{8}$ — $\frac{3}{4}$ — $\frac{7}{8}$ inch.
per piece.

SCRATCH AWLS.—Cast Steel.

No. 1, ... per gross,
 " 2, ...   "
 " 3, ...   "

POLISHED WROUGHT HAMMERS.

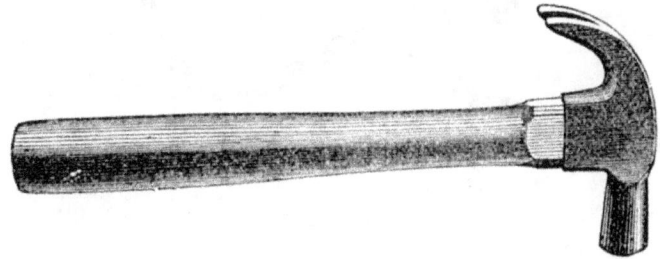

No. 1, ...   No. 2, ...

CAST STEEL DIVIDERS.

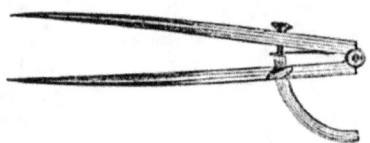

5 Inch, ...	per dozen,
6 "	"
7 "	"
8 "	"
9 "	"
10 "	"
12 "	"
15 "	"
18 "	"
24 "	"

CAST STEEL COMPASSES.

3 Inch, ...	per dozen,
4 "	"
5 "	"
6 "	"
7 "	"
8 "	"
9 "	"
10 "	"
12 "	"

CALIPERS.

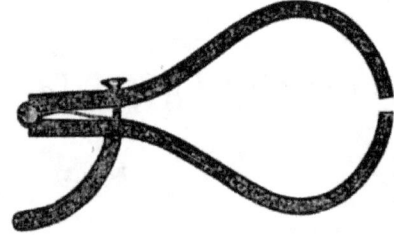

6 Inch, ...	per dozen,
8 "	"
10 "	"
12 "	"
15 "	"

STOW'S IMPROVED
PATENT ENCASED MACHINES.

O. W. STOW'S
PATENT ADJUSTABLE BAR FOLDER.

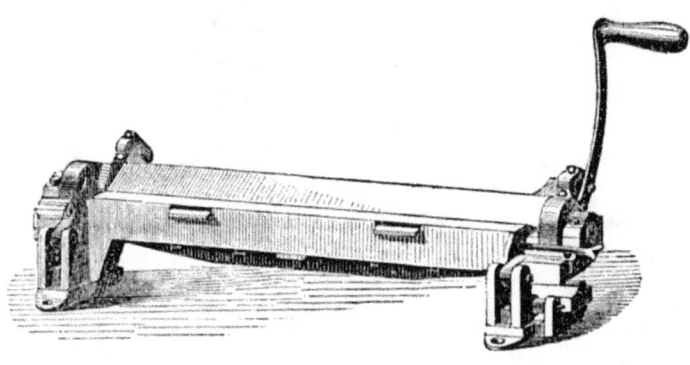

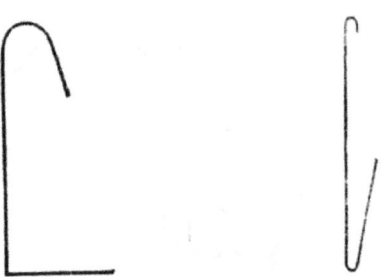

This simple and admirable machine is decidedly the best in use. It forms a square joint, turns a round edge for wiring, and forms locks on very heavy plate with ease.

No. 0, O. W. Stow's Patent of 1860, 22 inch, ... $18 00
    00,   "   "   "   "   17   " 13 50

IMPROVED GROOVING MACHINE.

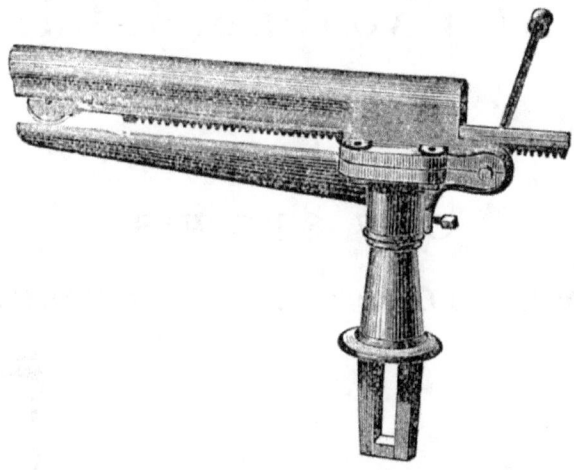

Common, 17 inch, ... $9 50, with Rotary Standard, ... $10 25
For Heavy Work, 20 inch . . 12 00, " " " 12 75

WIRING MACHINE.

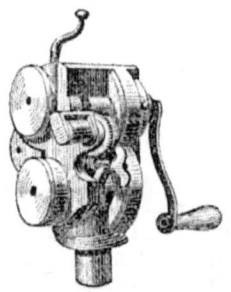

O. W. Stow's Patent, encased, . . $12 25, with Rotary Standard, . . $13 00

SETTING DOWN MACHINE.

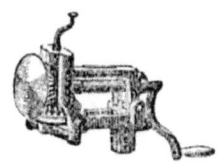

O. W. Stow's Improved, ... $8 50, with Rotary Standard, . . . $9 25

TURNING MACHINES.

WITH EXTRA FACES.

 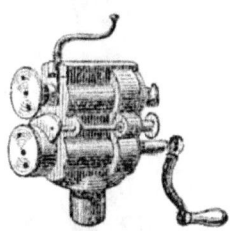

LARGE TURNING.   SMALL TURNING.

O. W. Stow's Patent encased, Large, . $9 75, with Rotary Standard, . $10 50
" " " " " Small, . 9 50, " " " . 10 25

BURRING MACHINES.

WITH EXTRA FACES.

LARGE BURRING.   **SMALL BURRING.**

O. W. Stow's Patent encased, Large Burr, $8 75, with Rotary Standard, $9 50
"   "   "   "   Small "   8 25, "   "   "   9 00

STANDARDS.

WIRING STANDARD.   **SMALL MEDIUM STANDARD.**

Wiring and Small Machine Standard, each 75 cents.

A Full Set of O. W. Stow's Patent Encased Machines is made up as follows:

O. W. Stow's Improved Adjustable Bar Folder, 22 in.,	$18 00	. . .		$18 00
" " Groover, 20 in.,	. .	12 00,	with stand,	12 75
" Patent Encased Wiring,	. . .	12 25,	"	13 00
" Improved Setting down,	. . .	8 50,	"	9 25
" Patent Encased Large Turning,	.	9 75,	"	10 50
" " " Small "	.	9 50,	"	10 25
" " " Large Burring,	.	8 75,	"	9 50
" " " Small "	.	8 25,	"	9 00
Full set.		$87 00,	"	$92 25
Full set with 14 inch Folder and 17 inch Groover,		$80 00,	"	$85 00

The following cuts and explanations will be of service to all using these Machines:

Stow's Patent Encased Machines, with Adjustable Boxes and Duplicate Parts.

The manner in which Tinners' Machines have heretofore been made, has caused all parties using them much vexation and expense, from the fact that the parts were not interchangeable. Hence, if any part of a machine was imperfect or failed, it could not be replaced without sending the entire machine to the manufacturer for repairs.

The need of machines made with different parts uniform and interchangeable, has long been apparent and after much expense the manufacturers have at last perfected machinery for so making the set of machines that all the parts of each machine are precisely alike, and all are perfect.

In addition to this, the patentee of O. W. Stow's Adjustable Bar Folder has invented and patented an adjustable Box, by means of which the upper face of each machine can be moved forward or backward. By these improvements the following advantages are secured:

I. All the parts being made by accurate machinery from perfect patterns, are perfect.

II. All parts of each machine are stamped with a letter or figure; if any part fails, all that is necessary is to write direct to us, giving the name of the machine cast upon the case, and the letter or number stamped upon the part, and a duplicate can be forwarded by mail or express.

III. The form of the machine is such that the gear is encased so as to keep it free from dirt. The boxes are well fitted, and oil holes are drilled. The journals are long to prevent wearing, and all parts are constructed of the best materials, and with the most thorough workmanship.

IV. By means of the adjustable box the upper faces of the machines can be moved backward or forward, to accommodate different thicknesses of tin, or to compensate for the wearing of the journals.

Below we give cuts of the different parts of the *Adjustable Box* and directions for adjusting, which will apply to the entire set, as the Adjustable Box is alike in all.

In these directions the machine is supposed to be placed on the standard with the crank to the right hand. The lower roller is always stationary, and the upper one adjustable by screwing the bearing F backward or forward through the rocking box E.

Before adjusting it, the set nut G should be loosened by placing the large wrench upon it with the handle up and turning toward you. Then to move the face forward, place the small wrench on F, with the handle up and turn from you; to move it back, put on the wrench in the same way, and turn toward you. After bringing the face to its proper position, the set nut G should always be screwed up against E, in order to keep the bearing F from being turned by the friction of the shaft. If the bearings of the upper shaft become worn so as to let the shaft slip backward and forward, loosen the screw in the clasp nut H, turn H over from you until it does not slip, then tighten the screw No. 5 again. When the boxes under the lower shaft wear down, they can be raised by means of the screw No. 3, under the frame A. All the other parts of the machine are substantially like the common ones, and will be understood by all tinners.

The machines can be readily taken apart by taking out the screw No. 2.

Please bear in mind that all these machines are warranted. Each one is carefully inspected before leaving the factory, and should any part break with fair usage, in consequence of undetected flaws in the steel, it will be replaced at our expense.

On page 167, we give cuts of the different parts of the Wiring Machine, with the letter or figure by which each part should be ordered.

The corresponding parts of other machines in the set bear the same letters or figures as far down as the letter O. Those bearing the letters from P to U, inclusive, are found only in the Wiring Machine.

List of Parts.

A   Frame.
B   Cap.
C   Upper Roller.
D   Lower   "
E   Rocking Box.
F   Rocking Box Bearing.
G   Set Nut on F.
H   Clasp Nut.

Journal Boxes.

I   Front Upper Box, for Upper Roller.
J   Front Lower   "   "   "   "
K   Front and Back Top Boxes for Lower Roller.
L   "   "   "   Lower "   "   "   "
M   Gears.
N   Sliding Gauge.
O   "   "   Nut.
P   Forming Gauge, for Wiring Machine.
Q   "   "   Roller, for Wiring Machine.
R   "   "   Worm Gear, for Wiring Machine.
S   "   "   Nut, for Wiring Machine.
T   Worm Gear Screw.
U   "   "   "   Holder.

Screws.

No. 1   Crank Screw.
    2   Cap   "
    3   Lower Box Screws.
    4   Worm Gear Screw Holder Bolt.
    5   Clasp Nut Screw.
——-   Spring.

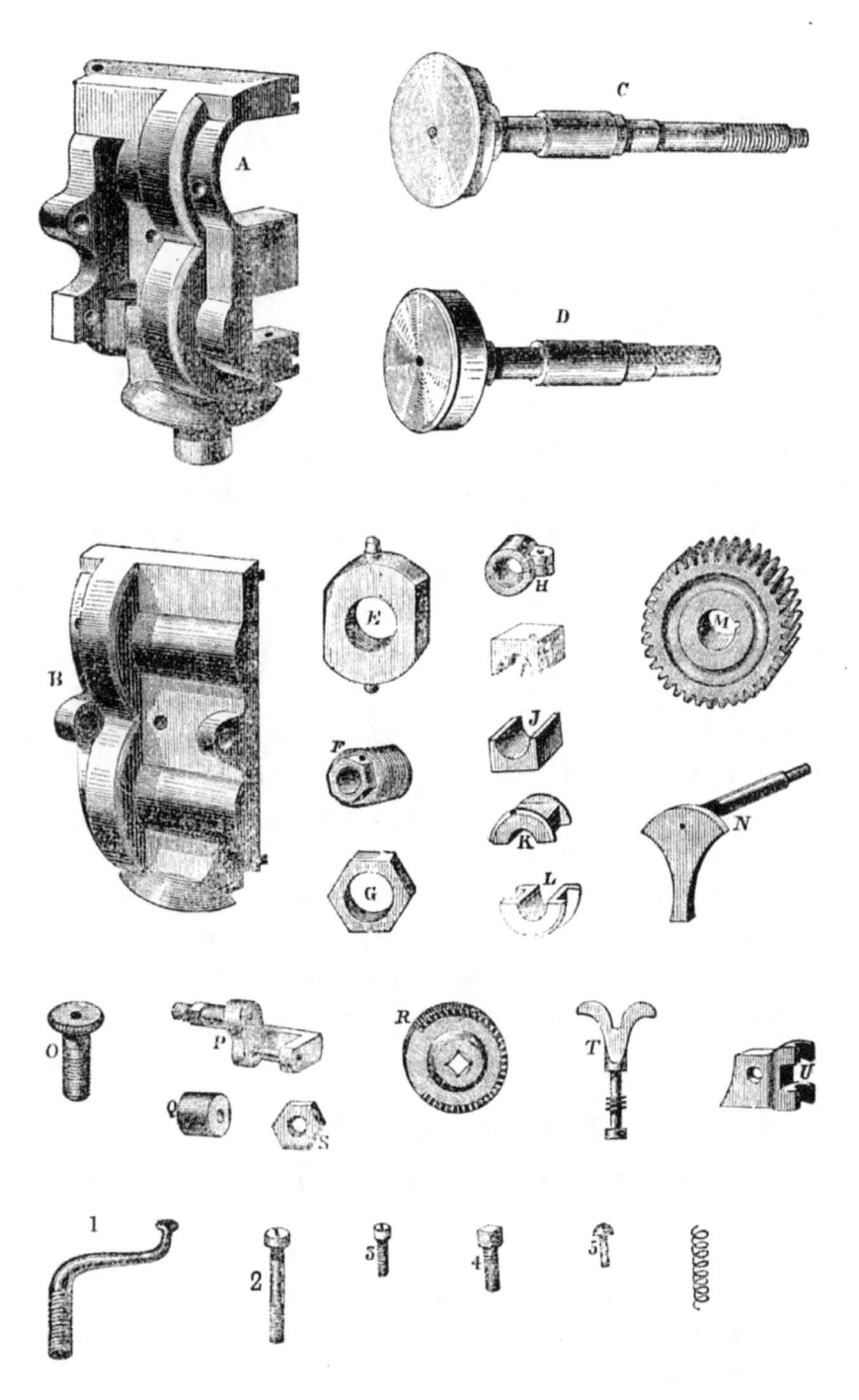

Directions for Using
O. W. STOW'S ADJUSTABLE BAR FOLDER.

Fasten the machine to a bench by means of small wood screws, with the crank at the right hand.

Place the edge of the sheet of tin under the folding plate, then bring over the folding bar, and the lock is formed. To form a bend at right angles, put the stop A in such a position as to stop the folding bar from turning more than one-quarter of a revolution.

It will be noticed that the folding bar is made in two parts, one of which is adjustable with reference to the folding plate, for the purpose of turning a close or open lock. This feature greatly increases the utility of the machine; for while it will do any work done by any other machine, and will form locks on heavy plate more easily than most other machines, it will at the same time turn the edges of a sheet of tin to fit wire of any size, so that it will take the place of the turning machines in wiring straight work.

To form a bend to fit wire of any size, set the folding bar so as to press more or less closely, when it is turned over on the plate; this is done by the thumb-screw at the right hand of the folding bar. By loosening this thumb-screw and moving from right to left, the folding bar is raised to form a close lock; by moving it from left to right it is put in position to form an open lock, and these changes can be made with great ease and rapidity. If the jaws do not hold the tin firmly, make them do so by turning the screws in the end of the frame that holds the friction rollers.

Tinsmiths will find it for their interest to purchase this folder.

Directions for Using
O. W. STOW'S IMPROVED GROOVING MACHINE.

This machine is operated like the common machines, but in changing the rollers, run the rack forward off the bar, and drive out the pin on which the roller turns.

In replacing the pin, be careful to make its ends agree or be even with the surface of the rack through which it passes.

INDEX.

A
Albata spoons, 55.
Animals, assorted, 92.
Antimony,

B
Babbit metal, 10.
Bake pans, hammered iron, 67.
Bake pans, polished, 102.
Banks, savings, 92.
Basin Bottoms 38.
Basin and pitcher, 79.
Basins, iron tinned, 104.
Basins, stamped tin, 46.
Basting spoons, 52.
Biscuit cutters, 49.
Biscuit pans, 113 to 115.
Black lead, 34.
Block tin, 8.
Boiler tops, 23.
Bottoms, copper, 22, 23.
Bottoms, metallic, 21, 22.
Bottoms, tin, 39.
Bow carts, 92.
Brass dipper bowls, 43.
Brass kettles, 19.
Brazier's solder, 10.
Bread pans, 49.
Britannia spoons, 54.
Britannia soup ladles, 108
Bucket covers, 38.
Buckets, covered, 88.
Bucket handles, 33.
Buckets, toy, 92.
Butter kettle covers, 41.
Butter kettles, toy, 92.
Burrs, 16.

C
Cake boxes, 82.
Cake cutters, 49.
Cake pans or moulds, 46.
Cake turners, 56.
Candle moulds, 41.
Candle mould pans and tips, 41.
Candlesticks, 87.
Candlestick bottoms, 40.
Canisters, 84, 85.
Can spouts, 20.
Can wax, 43.
Cash boxes, 82.
Castings, malleable, 24 to 26.
Chafing dishes, 51.
Chamber pails, 77, 97.
Chamber pail fixtures, 42.
Children's baths, 81.
Coal hods, 64.
Coffee mills, 60, 61.
Coffee pot handles, 19, 20.
Coffee pot stands, 66.
Coffee pot tops, 38.
Coffee and tea pot knobs, 31.
Coffee and tea pots, Britannia, 72.
Coffee and tea pots, planished, 70, 72.
Coffee and tea pots, tin, 68, 70.
Copper bolts and sheets, 8.
Copper bottoms, 22, 23.
Copper dipper bowls, 43.
Copper kettles, 19.
Cover litters, 64.
Corn cake pans, 116.
Cullenders, 103.
Cups, 116.
Cup dippers, 109, 110.

D
Dampers, 25.
Deed boxes, 83.
Dinner kettles, 119.
Dippers, 48.
Dipper bowls, brass and copper, 43.
Dippers, cup, 109, 110.
Dippers, flaring, 110, 111.
Dish covers, wire, 59.
Dish stands, 58.
Dish pans, 100.
Dredge or flour boxes, 90.
Dust pans, 89.

E
English hammered pans, 67.
Egg beaters, 50.
Egg stands, wire, 59.
Egg whips, 51.
Extinguishers, 29.

F
Fire carriers, 65.
Fire pots, 33.
Flaring dippers, 110.
Flat skimmers, 111.
Flesh forks, 112.
Flesh hooks, 113.
Flour or dredge boxes, 90.
Fluid cans, 41.
Fluted funnels, 51.
Foot tubs, 80.
Fork and spoon boxes, 85.
Forks, table, 53.
French stamped ware, 93 to 130.
French wash Basins, 104.
Fruit can tops and bottoms, 43.
Fruit can wax, 43.
Fry pans, French, 102.
Fruit or wash kettles, 98.
Fry pans, 66.
Funnel tubes, 29.

G
Galvanized hoop iron, 8.
Galvanized iron pipe, 12.
Grater blanks, 30.
Graters, 91.
Gravy strainers, 49, 119.
Gridirons, 103.

H
Handles, wood, 33.
Handle strainers, 58.
Hinges tin, 43.
Hip baths, 80.
Hoop iron, 7, 8.
Horns, 51.
House furnishing goods, 44 to 120.

I
Ice picks, 43.
Iron water and gas pipe, 12.
Isinglass, 28.

J
Jaggers, paste, 55.
Japanned tin ware, 73.
Japanned wash bowls, 90.
Jelly cake pans, 45.
Jelly moulds, 51.

K
Kettle ears, 17.
Kettle ears, cast iron, 26.
Knife and fork boxes, 85.
Knife trays, 86.
Kettles, 19, 99.

L

Ladles, 105 to 108.
Lamps and lanterns, 88.
Lanterns, 50.
Lead bars and pigs, 10.
Lead pipe and sheet lead, 11.

M

Machines and tools, 121 to 168.
Mallets 33.
Mashers. potatoe, 33.
Match safes, 91.
Melting ladles, 120,
Metallic bottoms, 21, 22.
Mica, 28.
Milk can handles, 26.
Milk pails, 97.
Milk skimmers, 113.
Muffin cups, 120.
Muffin pans, 114, 115.
Molasses cups, 90.
Money banks, 92.

N

Nursery lamps, 86.
Nutmeg graters, 91.

O

Oilers, 32.
Ornaments, 27.
Oval pans, 48.
Oyster blazers, 51.
Oyster ladles, 105.

P

Pail covers, 38.
Pans, stamped, 48.
Pan studs, 43.
Pastry jaggers, 55.
Patties, 47.
Pepper boxes, 90.
Perforated tin, 32.
Pipe rings, 43.
Plates, pie and dinner, 44, 45.
Pokers, 64.
Pot covers, 37.
Preserving kettles, 99.

R

Rattles and whistles, 92.
Rivets, 15, 16.
Rod iron, 8.
Rolling pins, 33.
Rosin, 33.
Round sieves, 120.

S

Sad irons. 65.
Sad iron stands, 65.
Sauce pans, 96.
Sauce pan handles, 18.
Savings banks, 92.
Scholars' companions, 92.
Scoops, 117, 118.
Screw tops, zinc. 30.
Shallow soup ladles, 105.
Sheet iron, American, 6.
Sheet iron, Galvanized, 7.
Sheet iron, Russia, 6.
Sheet lead and lead pipe, 11.
Shovels, 62, 63.
Sieves, 120.
Skimmers, deep, 106.
Skimmers, flat, 111.
Slop pails, 77.
Slop pail fixtures, 42.
Soap dishes, 51.
Solder, 10.
Soldering coppers, 29.

Soldering, iron handles, 33.
Soup ladles, 108.
Spelter, 10.
Spelter solder, 10.
Spice boxes. 83.
Spittoons. 89.
Spoons, 52 to 55.
Spouts. 20.
Sponging baths, 81.
Square pans, 49.
Stamped milk pans, 48.
Stamped and plain tin ware, 35 to 75.
Stamped tin'd iron ware, French, 93 to 120.
Steamer bottoms, 37.
Stew pans, 95.
Stove bolts, 17.
Stove ornaments, 27.
Stove polish, 34.
Strainers, wire, 57, 58.
Sugar bowls, 91.
Sugar boxes, 81.

T

Tea and coffee pot knobs, 31.
Tea and coffee strainers, 57.
Tea kettle breasts and covers, 40.
Tea kettles, 101.
Tea pot tops, 38, 39.
Tea pot handles, 19, 20.
Tin coffee pot bottoms, 39.
Tinned copper. 8.
Tinned castings, 24. 25, 26.
Tinned iron, 6.
Tinned iron ware, stamped, 92.
Tin pipe, 11.
Tin plate, 5, 6.
Tinners' furnishing supplies, 13.
Tin toys, japanned, 91, 92.
Toilet jar fixtures, 42.
Toilet bowls and pitchers, 79.
Toilet ware, 78, 79.
Toilet ware handles, 24.
Tools and machines, 121 to 168.
Toy buckets, 92.
Toy cups, 91.
Toy covered pails, 92.
Tumblers, 91.
Tumbler drainers, 86.
Trunks, 83.
Trunk, hoop iron, 8.
Turnbuckles and catches, 25.
Tureen covers, 41.

U V

Urn or faucet strainers, 57.
Vent nozzles,

W

Wash basins, iron tinned, 104.
Wash boiler covers, 23.
Wash bowls, tin. 46.
Wash kettles, 98.
Water coolers, 75, 76.
Water pails, japanned, 77.
Water pails, tinned iron, 98.
Wooden ware, 33.
Wire, annealed, 9.
Wire, bright, 9.
Wire, broom 10.
Wire, copper coated, 9.
Wire cloth, brass, 29.
Wire, tinned, English, 10.
Wire, galvanized with zinc, 9.
Wire goods, 57, 59.
Wire in stones, 9.

Z

Zinc nails, 10.
Zinc oilers, 32.
Zinc screw tops, 30.
Zinc sheets 8.

www.ingramcontent.com/pod-product-compliance
Lightning Source LLC
Chambersburg PA
CBHW060423010526
44118CB00017B/2330